MW01241089

Conscience and Power

The Contest for Civilization in the West

"Freedom is something one must feel and logic has no part in it. It is a privilege of noble minds which God has fitted to receive it, and it inspires them with a generous fervor."

— Alexis Charles Henri Clérel, Viscount de Tocqueville

Richard J. Bishirjian

En Route Books & Media, LLC
Saint Louis, MO

✸*ENROUTE*
Make the time

En Route Books and Media, LLC
5705 Rhodes Avenue
St. Louis, MO 63109

Contact us at contact@enroutebooksandmedia.com

Cover Credit: Avery Easter

Copyright 2023 American Academy of Distance Learning

Author Contact: Author Contact: Dr. Richard J. Bishirjian,
9466 Bay Front Drive, Norfolk, VA 23541 (757) 639-0470
cmpintl@yahoo.com

ISBN-13: 979-8-88870-043-3
Library of Congress Control Number: 2023936642

Dedicated to Richard V. Allen and Henry Kissinger

Table of Contents

Appendices

Acknowledgments

I am indebted to Dr. James Hannam, author of *God's Philosophers: How the Medieval World Laid the Foundations of Modern Science,* for reading my chapter on the Middle Ages and giving me the benefit of his vast knowledge of the Medieval era.

I am obliged also to thank the following for publishing chapters of *Conscience and Power* before the book itself found a publisher.

Chapter 2. Modern Political Religion. "Voegelinview." (October 23, 2018.) https://voegelinview.com/modern-political-religion

Chapter 5. Tocqueville's *L'Ancien régime et la revolution.* TheimaginativeConservative.org (December 15, 2019.)
https://theimaginativeconservative.org/2019/12/american-decline-what-to-do- richard-j-bishirjian.html

Chapter 5. Francis Graham Wilson's *Order and Legitimacy Modern Age* (Spring 2019), Vol. 61, No. 2, pp. 36-41. "Prelude to Civil War," Francis Graham Wilson on Spain."
https://isi.org/modern-age/prelude-to-civil-war-francis-graham-wilson-on-spain/

Chapter 5. Allan Bloom's *Closing of the American Mind* TheimaginativeConservative.org (November 1, 2018.) "Allan Bloom's Six Ways That Universities Corrupt the Youth."
https://theimaginativeconservative.org/2018/11/allan-bloom-closing-of-the-american-mind-universities-richard-bishirjian.html

Chapter 7. Closing of the American Soul to Religion TheimaginativeConservative.org (June 21, 2019.) "The Decline of Religious Colleges and Universities."
https://theimaginativeconservative.org/2019/06/decline-religious-colleges-universities-richard-bishirjian.html

Chapter 8. Recovery of Daimonic Souls from Disorder. "Voegelinview." (October 25, 2018.) "Conservatism and Spiritual and Social Recovery." https://voegelinview.com/author/cmpintl

Introduction

Conscience and Power examines how civilization in "the West" arose after the fall of the Roman Empire and has grappled ever after with a desire of citizens of nations of Western civilization for justice and the necessities of political order. This contest between Western man's sense of justice and the rule of nation states has had consequences for democracy in America and in the centers of Western Europe that explain the toxicity of modern social existence.

The author of *Conscience and Power* explores the theological and philosophical basis of Western civilization in the truths revealed to the mystics of ancient Israel and discovered by the philosophers of ancient Greece and Rome, truths that have found their expression in the Christian tradition. His purpose in making this inquiry is to ask what weaknesses of intellectual culture in the West have contributed to the fragility of popular government in the 21st century.

What is the basis of our consciousness of justice, what forces have shaped it and contributed to the character of democracy in the modern world? Are there solutions—improvements even—that can preserve democracy in the 21st century?

Conscience and Power, based on the author's years of teaching and writing on Western political philosophy, examines the fragility and possible failure of democracy in the 21st century. What we in the West inherited from ancient Israel, Greece, and Rome, which brought about an enduring Christendom, is no longer central to the lives of citizens of Western nation states.

Because the death of everything living is preceded by a natural process of birth, growth, and senescence, *Conscience and Power* asks how much longer democracies can live in the West before they, too, meet their end.

The suggestion that democracy is dying contains an observation and a judgment. We observe that everything around us ultimately dies, so it follows that even the civilization of the West will also die.

1

But, that observation contains a judgment that Western civilization is dying—now—from *self-inflicted* wounds. Are those wounds endemic to all civilizations and to democracies? What is it about democratic regimes that leads them to self-destruction, to suicide? How does this condition come about and, can this condition be remedied?

We, the citizens of the United States and Europe, are the heirs and stewards of Western culture, inhabiting patterns of thought, living, faith, tradition, and ritual handed down to us from the legacy of ancient Rome. Given our inheritance of every glory of "the West," we might assume we have learned something from it.

We learned, for example, that it took about a thousand years for the city of Rome to grow a republic, transform into an empire, and fall. And it took about five hundred years from the fall of Rome to the reestablishment of civilization in the West, what historians call "first Europe."

How, if we study the history of Rome or ancient Greece, can we avoid the same fate as the Romans and the Greeks? That was a question asked by the framers of the Constitution of the United States, who, following their studies of the history of ancient Rome and the cities of ancient Greece, designed a Constitution on principles that limit the powers of a government they hoped would assure its survival.

The American "founding generation" studied well and shaped the thirteen former English colonies from a community of disparate States into a Nation. The Framers sought a government that deterred the misuse of power and directed power to good ends. They understood also that man's fallen nature required that power be checked and that those institutions of government granted power must be balanced by competing powers. Underlying this mechanical concept of checks and balances was a homogeneous spiritual community of Protestant Christians shaped by historical events in England that drove them to the American colonies.

That history of England is filled with tension between the ruler and those ruled. It includes internecine fighting among the nobility that resulted in the Magna Carta, growing tension between Church and State and religious wars within the State, regicide in the execution of Charles I and the subsequent authoritarian rule by Oliver Cromwell, restoration of the monarchy and the deposing and replacing of another king in a "Glorious Revolution" that affirmed limits on the English monarchy and assured the growth of representative government.

Relations between England and the American colonists were irreparably injured by Britain's treatment of the American colonials during and after the French and Indian War, and that assured that the colonists would seek their independence from the British Crown. That led to the founding of an independent United States that is now—almost two hundred and fifty years later—showing signs of significant decline. That decline was preceded by disruptions of civil society in England, France, Germany, and Spain.

To be perfectly clear, we argue that American political culture is experiencing similar disorders caused, we believe, by its abandonment of the Western philosophical and theological traditions that once shaped what had come to be called "Christendom."

In establishing the fundamental law of American national government, the U.S. Constitution, the founding fathers did the best they could with materials that were at hand. Those materials included concepts of law, historical experience, religious history, and philosophical concepts that met the exigencies of their times. But by 1787, the influence of the Enlightenment had transmitted not only those practical concepts of organization and powers, but also viruses that threaten civil society hundreds of years later. Today, American democracy is dealing with the symptoms of the cancers those viruses have caused.

During and after the American Civil War, the homogeneous community of Protestant Christians throughout the United States was shaken by both the brutality of the war and the scientific theories that cast doubt on Christian revelation. American colleges and universities that once cherished their responsibility to transmit their Protestant faith and knowledge of Western civilization became handmaidens of the State. An American centralized, bureaucratic, administrative State came into existence that too often subverted the consent of the governed through government by special interests and deep state politics.

Some evidence includes the following: College educated citizens who know nothing of their history and celebrities who never studied government, history, economics, or foreign policy feel qualified to seek public office. American society is besieged by claims to government largess and of "rights" to engage in actions that America's religious culture rejected centuries ago and rejects still. Islamic radicals who believe that the West's culture is degenerate have fashioned an ideology that justifies murder and terror, and the government's response to the war against Islamic "terrorism" is to justify violation of the privacy of American citizens in the conduct of that war.

This reading of the decline of democratic politics in the 21st century, if accurate, could not have been predicted in 1787, but something like it was feared. Educated colonists of what came to be called the "founding generation" of mid-18th century America had read ancient history, law, and philosophy and knew that rule by masses of uneducated "citizens" who cared for pleasure absent of civic responsibility was the downfall of what ancient Greeks and Romans called "democracy." Fortunately for the ancient Greeks and Romans, periodically, but only in times of crisis, great men rose to meet the needs of their days and restored order.

Historical timelines can be useful in understanding, not merely justifying, that statement. They can show epochal moments when there was an upward or downward motion that had a definitive beginning and ending. The timeline traveled in this book provides a sense that American democracy has reached its end along with the life of a nation whose mores, philosophical traditions, Constitution, and laws for almost two hundred and fifty years have nourished and supported a traditional order of society.

Our understanding of whether the American nation—or the democracies of England, France, Germany or Spain—has a future depends on whether we have the stomach to engage in a review of what the traditional order of the West is and of which of its disorders have driven us to ask if our sense of an ending is imagined or real. Our friends, the citizens of the nations of Europe who sensed the demise of their democracies decades ago, will sympathize with us.

In Europe, furthermore, the slowing of the birthrate among Christians is increasing the influence of non-Christian populations whose higher birthrates and increasing immigration into European Union States challenge European cities to maintain order. European political leaders who act as if they consider Europe's Christian traditions *equal* to the traditions of all other civilizations, including those that embraced Islam, have aroused a resurgent nationalism.

Europe, buffeted by a bullying Russian kleptocracy and organized into a fractious "European Union," has ceased to lead the West in international affairs and is fast becoming insignificant in terms of geopolitical power. Western European cities, as a result, are becoming significant only as interesting tourist destinations.

This realignment has not escaped Russia's attention, and post-Soviet Russian leaders are slowly attempting to absorb the former satellites of the Soviet Union into Russia's sphere of influence. Russia will strive to make Ukraine, the Baltic states—every nation formerly dominated by the former Soviet Union—subjects of Russia's kleptocracy. Only insofar as a rising Islam and a powerful China challenge Russia will the United States and Russia discover a mutuality of interests.

Where does that leave the United States? In one word—vulnerable. Vulnerable to Islamic terrorists, vulnerable to an electorate ill-educated for an economy that relies less on manufacturing and more on technological skills, vulnerable to wage stagnation, vulnerable to moral decline, and vulnerable to all the weaknesses of democracies.

The great promises of an independent American democratic republic, such as individual liberty, freedom of enterprise, constitutional limits on government power, and the rule of law, have been called into question. No viable community of belief exists to secure either the blessings of American liberty in a dangerous world or the promise of American power in a destabilized Western Europe.

The observation that, after a prolonged period of drought, we should ask, "Is this a desert?" raises the question of whether deeper problems, ones turning on the nature of Western civilization itself, are at work. They compel us to look at our present condition and engage in a philosophical re-examination of the intellectual foundations of the West. If we do so, though, who will engage in these philosophical discussions? Our college educated citizens have lost, or never learned, philosophy as a way of discovery of truth. All is relative, they are taught, and many have come to believe.

The method employed in this book, therefore, runs counter to the normal way that we address these political problems—by ignoring them. Here, in *Conscience and Power*, we explore our current dilemma by reference to the history of Western philosophy and civilization and the knowledge that the life of all nations participates in transcendent divine reality—that is, in the life of God. In Chapter 11, "Recovery of Daimonic Souls from Disorder," for instance, we examine the mystic character of the life of the American nation and the conscience of the West.

In search of solutions, therefore, we bring to bear on the questions asked here all that we know and were taught about religion and philosophy, the civilization of the West, and Western culture. Our search is assisted by similar assessments, in addition to our own, to explain the dangers that democracy inflicts on the American people and the disorders and unrest in civil society democratic rule can create.

The author of this study brings to this task a career as a college teacher and an education entrepreneur. He learned classical political theory from scholars at the University of Notre Dame, many of whom were émigrés from Western Europe in World War II. In addition to teaching courses in political theory, modern ideology, American national government, and Constitutional Law, he answered the call of service in the Reagan Administration, served on a Transition Team in the Office of the President-Elect, and accepted a nomination to a sub-cabinet post at the United States International Communication Agency.

This author has written a great deal about a public philosophy that informs American democracy with insight into discoverable, public truths that have guided American politics from its beginning.[1] Such public philosophy can be seen in his 2015 study entitled *The Conservative Rebellion*[2] where he argued that the United States is the beneficiary of a sustained tradition of rebellion—not revolution. The spirit of that rebellion engendered America's independence from Britain and has risen at critical times in our history when it seemed that democracy in America was on the wrong track.

Such rebellion, however, has been hampered by a "Left University" system that dominates American colleges and universities on which we rely for education and intentionally denies to generations of students' knowledge of fundamental truths that have sustained democracy in America since the first colonists arrived in the New World. Since the late 1960s, our secondary schools, colleges, and universities have abdicated their responsibility to educate our citizens as integral to a self-governing democratic republic.

So, here we looked for others who sought answers to problems of political order in the West and found these three persons who

---

[1] Richard Bishirjian, *A Public Philosophy Reader* (New Rochelle: Arlingtonn House, 1978).

[2] Richard Bishirjian, *The Conservative Rebellion* (South Bend: St. Augustine's Press, 2015).

authored four books that we examine here:

1.   Alexis de Tocqueville, *Democracy in America* (1835) and
     The Old Régime and the French Revolution (1856)
2.   Francis Graham Wilson, *Order and Legitimacy* (1967)
3.   Allan Bloom, *The Closing of the American Mind* (1987)

The 19th-century French political theorist, writer, and politician, Alexis Charles Henri Clérel, Viscount de Tocqueville (1805-1859), is probably best known for his *Democracy in America*. But his *Recollections* that tell us something about his life and career is of value as is the second volume of *Democracy in America*. What Tocqueville had to say about America in 1831, when he and a colleague traveled throughout the United States, expresses insights into the nature of American democracy that are true today and sometimes unpleasant to American ears.

In addition to Tocqueville, we will consider what Professor Francis Graham Wilson (1901-1976) had to say. Wilson did not promote his scholarship, so his insights have been long forgotten. But half a century ago, this erudite political philosopher examined the condition of American civil society by comparing it to 19th- and 20th-century Spain. Spanish traditionalists addressed problems in Spain's civil society from the invasion of Spain by Napoleon in 1808 through the military regime of Francisco Franco, and Wilson thought he saw something familiar.

A Catholic, raised in Texas where he became fluent in Spanish, Wilson spent time in Spain and saw that problems affecting civil society in that country were quite similar to our own. Since long simmering issues in Spain were resolved in civil war and in the imposition of an authoritarian regime, a review of Wilson's thought compels us to ask how similar are conditions in the United States in the 2020's to conditions in Spain in the 1930's?

We'll also look at the 1987 book *The Closing of the American Mind* by political theorist Allan Bloom (1930-1992), who indicts modern education for impoverishing our souls. Bloom's book shook the foundations of American higher education and is an enduring testament to political thinkers who studied with Leo Strauss at the University of Chicago. There in the American Midwest the life of the mind was supported by Jewish *émigrés* who came to Chicago from Russia after the Bolshevik Revolution, made successful careers, and financially supported the University of Chicago.

As we shall see from examining Alexis de Tocqueville, Francis Graham Wilson and Allan Bloom, we are not the first to ask if democracy in the West is nearing its end.

1

How We Got Here

In the modern era, four ideologies infected civilization in the West with destructive effect. These are namely:

1. *L'Esprit révolutionnaire* of the French Revolution in the 18th century;
2. the German Idealism of Fichte, Hegel, Schiller and its American variant, "Transcendentalism;"
3. the atheist humanism of Karl Marx; and
4. the "positivism" of August Comte in the 19th century.

It took many years to diagnose these ideologies properly, but not before the *Ancien Régime* of France was destroyed and what came to be understood as "totalitarian" movements arising out of the first world war overtook Russia, Germany, and Italy, threw Western Europe into a second world war, and submerged the United States in military engagements in Korea and Vietnam. Because of the depth of this disorder of the human spirit, which political theorists have identified as a political "religion," it is impermeable to rational argument.

Once the acolytes of these four ideologies gain control of nations, they can be countered only by force of arms. Before then, entire nations may be saved from disaster only by educating their intelligentsia, those most susceptible to the disease of political religion, about the dangers they pose. If control of education falls, therefore, into the hands of persons influenced by political religion, every effort must be directed at recovery.

Today, that recovery requires us to understand where we were *before* we got to this point of decline in intellectual culture in the West. We begin that intellectual journey toward recovery by examining the influence in the West of ancient Israel, Greece, and Rome, of Christianity, and of the birth in the Middle Ages of a new civilization called Christendom.

From Ancient Israel to "First Europe" and the Middle Ages

The philosophical and theological traditions of the West are little known because the ancient tribes that shaped civilization after the fall of the Roman empire have become secular nation-states. The foundations for that secularization were laid during what we call the "late Middle Ages," and the nations of Western Europe from the Renaissance through today struggle to affirm what once shaped a common "consciens," or common sense amongst their citizens.

As evidence of the "common" aspect of "consciens" or *conscience*, a digital "Wiktionary" search reveals that many nations in the West have a word for it:

- Catalan: conscient
- French: conscient
- Italian: cosciente
- Portuguese: consciente
- Romanian: conștient
- Spanish: consciente

In German, the word is *Gewissen*, to have a clear or guilty conscience.

That commonality of experience expressed in language was based on the Christian faith, which shaped a common understanding of the West. After nearly eleven hundred years since the new world of "first Europe" was shaped in the 10th century, however, we are to the point of characterizing our times as "post-Christian." Here, therefore, is a much needed and useful summary of what once constituted the philosophical and theological basis of the West.

Ancient Israel

We have engaged in a political journey of such length and complexity—from Philadelphia in 1787 through the destruction of Western Europe in two world wars in the 20th century—that it confuses us and makes it difficult to understand how we got here. The "classical" learning of the best-educated Americans like James Madison, who entered the College of New Jersey in 1769, or Thomas Jefferson, who entered the College of William and Mary in 1759, has been discarded. Thus, what was once called a "classical" education has not been imparted to succeeding generations.

Even if that tradition had continued, few would have the intellectual ability to transcend the allure of the French *philosophes* of the 18th-century, the German idealists of the 19th-century, or the Communist ideologues of the 20th-century. Much later, the flow to the United States of classically trained émigré scholars in the mid-20th century from the totalitarian movements in Europe led to the recovery of the philosophical ground of the West in the classical philosophy of ancient Hellas. To that understanding, Eric Voegelin recovered for American political theorists an appreciation of the revelation to Israel by Yahweh.

Protestant Christians in the early years of the American colonies had read the Old Testament and appreciated the encounter of the ancient tribes of Israel with Yahweh. And these educated colonists were also taught the political theory of Marcus Tullius Cicero along with a smattering of ideas from the philosophy of Socrates, Plato, and Aristotle. Unfortunately, that knowledge resides in very few places in America today. It was sufficient, however, in the 18th century to give us independence from England and a constitutionally-based form of limited government. Today, even in those places where this achievement is remembered, we struggle to find talented minds to articulate its truths.

Such a heritage from ancient Israel is an important part of the

lives of Protestant, Catholic, and Jewish Americans,[1] for it binds us
to a common experience of God's intervention in history. That experience, which is lost amidst our secularism, is, nonetheless, central to who we Americans are today and from whence we came. In
short, the civilization of the West in general, and American culture
in particular, is rooted in the encounter of the ancient tribes of Israel with Yahweh and, for non-Jews, includes a commonly shared
morality based on God's commandments—again, God's intervention in history.

Christians may not understand the wonderful sophistication of
Jewish tradition as it searches for moral truth, but if we are to sustain Western culture, we must recover that sense of amazement and
wonder that these truths are not our creations, but God's. Putting
that tradition back into American higher education must involve a
recovery of our shared experience of God's intervention in history.

That intervention is part of our understanding of ourselves as
participants in a defining historical moment of the Hebrew clans
when, as reported in Exodus (19:1), Moses ascended the holy
mountain of Sinai and experienced the presence of God. Moses'
experience of Yahweh finds a parallel in an earlier theophany[2] experienced by Abram after his victory in battle with Chedorlaomer.

The king of Sodom, whose kingdom had been saved by Abram,
offered to reward him for his victory. Abram replied that he had
sworn to Yahweh that he would not take even the smallest token of
reward for the victory. If he did, the king of Sodom would take
credit for the good fortune of Abram when in truth Yahweh was
responsible. The book of Genesis 15 reports as follows: "Some

---

[1] I was privileged to have studied with Eric Voegelin at the University
of Notre Dame and attend his class during a semester he taught at the
University of Dallas, and with scholars influenced by him, especially Gerhart Niemeyer. My understanding of the importance of ancient Israel was
developed by my Lutheran upbringing and confirmed by reading Voegelin's *Order and History, Vol. 1, Israel and Revelation* (Baton Rouge: Louisiana
State University Press, 1958).

[2] A theophany is an experience of God's presence.

time after these events, this word of the Lord came to Abram in a vision: 'Fear not, Abram! I am your shield; I will make your reward very great!'" (15:1).[3]

A theophany of Yahweh, then, which comforted Abram in a moment of great political danger, also shaped the political existence of the Hebrew clans after their escape from Egypt. On a holy mountain, Moses experienced the voice of Yahweh which told him: "If you hearken to my voice and keep my covenant, you shall be my special possession, dearer to me than all other people, though all the earth is mine. You shall be to me a kingdom of priests, a holy nation" (Exodus 19:5-6).

The conflicts of Abram and Moses with the dominant political units of the ancient Near East were grounded in theophanies which they interpreted as promises: to Abram that his "reward" will be "great" and to Moses the conditional promise that "If you hearken to my voice and keep my covenant, you shall be my special possession." This promise to Moses is a "Covenant" with a community which is a "possession" of God by virtue of its possession of a new truth about God.

To be sure, others in the ancient Near East claimed to be the recipient of favors of a god. The Babylonian Nabonidus, for example, had a stela inscribed commemorating his ascendance to power as the reward of the moon-god, Sin.

> "At midnight he (Sin) made me have a dream and said (in the dream) as follows:
> 'Rebuild speedily Ehulhul, the temple of Sin in Harran, and I will hand over to you all the countries.'"[4]

But the theophany of Sin with Nabonidus is distinguishable from

---

[3] All Biblical quotations are taken from the *New American Bible* (New York: P. J. Kenedy & Sons, 1970).

[4] James B. Pritchard, ed. *Ancient Near Eastern Texts Relating to the Old Testament* (Princeton: Princeton University Press, 1969), 562.

the covenant of Yahweh with Abram and Moses because Nabonidus' god, Sin, was a cosmological divinity, and the mode of cosmological kingship characteristic of the ancient Near East remained intact.

The Israelite theophany, however, created a new political consciousness. Through their response to the revelation of the transcendent Yahweh, the Hebrew clans became a new people in history, a theopolity ordered under fundamental rules emanating from a transcendent, not cosmological, Yahweh. In Exodus 3, Moses encounters the presence of Yahweh, not as an intracosmic divinity but as transcendent divine reality. From the burning bush, Yahweh reveals his name, "I am who I am," a concept which breaks the cosmological association of the gods with the divine cosmos.

In Judges 5, also, Yahweh is described not in the mode of an intracosmic divinity, but as divine reality whose presence is manifest in natural phenomena:

> O Lord, when you went out from Seir, when you marched from the land of Edom, the earth quaked and the heavens were shaken, while the clouds sent down showers. Mountains trembled in the presence of the Lord, the One of Sinai, in the presence of the Lord, the God of Israel. (Judges 5:4-5).

Through their response to this revelation, the Hebrew clans who concluded the covenant with Yahweh became a new people in history. The people of Israel were conscious of their "history" as the record of those moments in which the God of Israel revealed Himself to them by his creative acts.

> Ask now of the days of old, before your time, ever since God created man upon the earth; ask from one end of the sky to the other: Did anything so great ever happen before? Was it ever heard of? Did a people ever hear the voice of God speaking from the midst of a fire, as you did and live?

Or did any god venture to go and take a nation for himself from the midst of another nation, by testing, by signs and wonders, by war, with his strong hand and outstretched arm, and by great terrors, all of which the Lord, your God, did for Egypt before your very eyes? (Deut. 4:32-34)

Though the covenant between God and Hebrew tribes shaped the nation of Israel, a mystery of participation in divine reality also shaped Christian civilization in the West because divine reality cannot be manifest fully in one historical culture.

There is a tension in the covenant formula between pragmatic political existence and political existence transformed by right relationship to God. Throughout the early history of Israel, Israel's consciousness of itself as the people of God runs counter to the necessities of pragmatic political existence.

The need to go to war in order to free themselves from servitude to the Canaanites, reported in Judges 5, for example, becomes, later in the imperial history of Israel, the need to go to war, not for the compelling reasons of a holy war, but because in spring all kings commence their campaigns (2 Sam. 11:1).

The idea that there is that which belongs to man, and that which is God's, shaped the West and our appreciation of the ancient Greeks and the contest between conscience and power, which is central to the meaning of our examination.

Ancient Greece

The citizens of the ancient city-states of Hellas that we collectively call "Greece" were very different from us. But many educated men in Western Europe, and many in colonial Virginia and New England, were classically trained,[5] absorbed in the truths discovered by the ancient Greeks. Those who were not sought from those

---

[5] Carl J. Richard, *The Founders and the Classics: Greece, Rome, and the American Enlightenment* (Harvard University Press, 1994).

who were the knowledge of important lessons from the Greeks. Here is how John Adams explained the principles of American resistance to the British Crown: "These are what are called revolution-principles. They are the principles of Aristotle and Plato, of Livy and Cicero, of Sydney, Harrington and Lock."[6]

Solon

The ideas of another important statesman of Athens, Solon, was found to be of interest to American colonists. Americans in 1776 and 1781 understood themselves to be performing Solon-like roles as statesmen of an American republic yet to come into existence.

Solon (594 BC) was a nobleman and leader of his fellow Athenians who reformed Athenian politics by tying the holding of political office to differentiated degrees of property. Thus, Solon gave every citizen a stake in the existing political order. He cancelled debts and freed Athenians who had been enslaved. The lowest, laboring class, could not hold office, but they were permitted to vote in the Assembly and act as jurors in courts of law. By means of these reforms, Solon sought to instill a sense of duty in all the citizens of Athens and punished those who disengaged from politics with loss of citizenship.

Solon stood at the height of the history of Athens when the citizens of Athens accepted his noble leadership. But his regime was followed by the tyrant Peisistratus (561 BC), an invasion by Sparta which in turn was followed by the democratic reforms of Cleisthenes (508/7 BC).

Americans of the 18th century who read Plutarch, Polybius, and Thucydides understood the weaknesses of democratic regimes and were committed not to make the same mistakes in America. In addition to Solon, therefore, when 18th-century American colonists wanted to understand the weaknesses of various types of regimes,

---

[6] Ibid., 232.

they read Aristotle's *Politics*, Book VI of Polybius' *Histories*, and some aspects of Plato's *Republic*.

But the leading men in the American colonies appreciated more Plato's account of the tragic death of Socrates than Plato's Myth of the Cave or Aristotle's concept of right by nature. And when they sought understanding of immutable natural law, they turned to an ancient Roman, Marcus Tullius Cicero. The immense influence of ancient Greek philosophy would come later, in the mid-20th century, when classical scholarship was carried to the shores of America by émigrés fleeing totalitarian ideologues in Europe.

Aristotle

Aristotle, another source of inspiration for America's "Founding" generation, gave them insight into the nature of political order, types of constitutions, and the systematic inquiry into the best regime and the study of ethics. Books 3, 4 and 5 of his *Politics* contain what today we understand as the beginning of the study of comparative government or constitutions.

The word "constitution" in classical Greek is *politeia* and each *politeia* is defined by a dominant social class. In democracies, the people are dominant. In oligarchies, the few. But a right *politeia* is one that directs itself to a common good, what we today call "the public interest." This common good does not consist solely in material goods but is concerned with virtue and vice and the order of the soul.

The best *politeia* is defined by the best men (*aristoi*). But Aristotle calls our attention to something that he calls the best *politeia* absolutely. Statesmen (lawgivers) must keep this best *politeia* in mind before they examine all the variants of *politeia* in order to design the best and most practicable laws.

In Book 4, Aristotle concludes that the most practicable *politeia* is the middle class *politeia*. A middle class *politeia* is dominated by neither the very rich nor the very poor, but by those of moderate means. The middle classes, he observes, are least inclined to shun office, and they are equal and alike one to another. Friendship is most likely to exist under such conditions, and this *politeia* will be free from faction.

In Book 5, Aristotle explores the origins of *politeia* in social agreement or consensus about what is just. Democracy originates in equality in all things. Oligarchy consists of those who are unequal in property. In time, a class war originates and faction ensues in disagreements about what is just.

Each type of constitution has its weaknesses. The weakness of democracy is revealed in the insolence of demagogues who cause property owners to band together. The weakness of oligarchies is revealed when people are treated unjustly and the honors of office are shared only by the few. The weakness of aristocracies is revealed when the few share in honors and the wealthy men who hold office behave insolently and use their offices for personal gain. Tyranny occurs when a demagogue suppresses the nobles. Aristocracy, Aristotle observes, seeks the good of the people, but tyranny seeks no common good.

These were important lessons that the Framers of the Constitution took to heart.

Plato

In the ancient world, individuals understood themselves in terms of their citizenship. Socrates took pride in his duties as a citizen-soldier and was known for his obedience to the laws of Athens. Even when sentenced to death, Socrates did not seek exile, but carried out the sentence by taking a drink of poison hemlock.

Socrates' tragic death had enormous impact on his student, Plato, who made the *persona* of Socrates a central figure in his philosophical dialogues. Plato's Academy, or school, became the model for education in which a philosopher engages his students with questions and discussions about reality, including *to on*, divine being.

Plato's method of education, what the Greeks called *paidaiea*, focused on a teacher who knows something and transmits that knowledge in ways of engagement that become a part of the character of his students. As such, the purpose of *paidaiea* is education of the character of citizens, not the learning of skills. Today much of what passes for higher education is training in skills, or vocations, and too much of what is taught in the humanities and social sciences today hides a disposition to reject the obligations of citizenship.

In colonial America, a few fortunate students studied these subjects in college. At the College of New Jersey (later named Princeton), President John Witherspoon, a classical scholar, taught moral theology greatly influenced by Plato and Aristotle. One of Witherspoon's students was James Madison. And at William and Mary in Virginia, Thomas Jefferson was introduced to the world of science and classical liberalism by William Small.

Still, classical Greek philosophy, which had been lost by the late 19th century as "Progressives" gained popularity, did not begin a recovery in America until the 20th century when émigré classical scholars such as Werner Jaeger, Eric Voegelin, Hannah Arendt, Leo Strauss, and others published works that now shape our understanding of the philosophical principles of political order.

That being the case, what can be learned from this historical experience with kingships, aristocracies, democracies, and tyrannies and from the many wise men of this ancient culture who warned their fellow citizens of the dangers that were to come?

The greatest period of ancient Athens is associated with Pericles (c. 495-429 BC) who, in less than fifteen years between 443 BC and 429 BC, oversaw an eruption of regenerative insights by Greek tragedians, namely, Aeschylus (c. 525-455 BC), Sophocles (497-406 BC), Euripides (c. 480-406 BC), and Aristophanes (446-386 BC), and historians, namely, Herodotus (450-420 BC), Thucydides (460-c. 395 BC), and Xenophon (c. 430-354 BC). Not to be overlooked were the philosophers, namely, Protagoras (490-420 BC), Hippias (460-399 BC), and, the greatest of them all, Socrates (469-399 BC). At the height of the glory of ancient Greece, Hellas was home, then, to some of the greatest inquiring minds in the history of the West.

Dramas that touched the soul, comedies that challenged the powerful, and the questioning of Socrates in search of truth, however, could not deter the collapse of Athenian social order. And in 399 BC, a sentence of death was imposed on Socrates by a democratic regime in Athens.

Despite accomplishments of lasting value during the Periclean Age, five hundred years before—in 9th century BC—Homer composed stories of Greek heroes that revealed ancient Greek culture had lost a ruling principle, a controlling source of order. The gods of ancient Greek religion were symbolic of social and spiritual disorder. What ancient Israel had, what truths Plato and Aristotle demonstrated, and which the Christian Gospels gave to the ancient world, ancient Greek religion lacked.

Students who read Homer's *Iliad* today will be amused by the *cosmos* of Greek gods, their actions, and how they manipulated the lives of the ancient Hellenes. But that modern amusement misses the disorder that shaped the lives of those ancient Hellenes.

From the perspective of 21st century America, it is very difficult for us to appreciate that for tens of thousands of years before Israel's encounter with Yahweh and the breakthrough of Greek natural philosophy in the 7th century BC, and their successors Socrates, Plato and Aristotle, ancient man had a very limited understanding of himself as a unity of body and soul.

What we take for granted about the human *psyche* was for millennia quite limited. Consciousness of the soul's depth would begin only in the discovery in the 6th and 5th century by Greek natural philosophers (*physiologoi*) who sought to know the origin (*arche*) of being (*to on*) and being things (*ta onta*). We now group them as the "Presocratics."

Ancient man did not see the world around him as a universe of differentiated objects, but as a cosmos composed of other beings whose living presence was manifest in the progress of daily life. The elements of natural phenomena of a thunderstorm were not perceived, for example, as differentiated "natural" phenomena. A thunderstorm was a "storm god." The cosmos itself, earth, sea, heavens, winds, rivers, etc., were gods. Everywhere ancient man turned, he encountered the gods of the cosmos and interpreted his own actions by reference to their decisions.

Political order was also understood as existing in direct relationship with the cosmic gods. Human order was not an order which was autonomous or independent of an order higher than itself. Rather, it was perceived as an extension of cosmic order populated by gods. Political community, therefore, was experienced as a smaller portion of a larger sacred order or cosmos. As such, Eric Voegelin has called this view "microcosmic" and the form in which it was expressed he called the "cosmological myth."

The makers of these "cosmological" myths attempted to depict as best they could the relationship of man himself to a sacred cosmos, its origins, and the relationship of this original creation to political community. Cosmological "creation myths" explained not only the origin of the cosmos, but also the origin of political order.

The great legacy which we inherited from ancient Greece begins with Homer's introduction of the *psyche* (soul) as a force of order and Hesiod's depiction of order as rising from chaos by the act of Zeus. Heraclitus enlarged the concept of an ordered soul, and Greek tragedians, Aeschylus and Sophocles, focused on this spiritual force in conflict with the disorder of gods.

Socrates countered the Sophistic notion that "man is the measure of all things" by evoking the ordering experience of divine reality. Clearly, Greek history moved in the direction of greater, differentiated, understanding of order and its origin in responsive souls to divine reality.

In order to appreciate how different Plato's teachings were from mythic thought, we'll take a brief look at his Myth of the Cave found in Book Seven of his *Republic*.

Here are key pages of Plato's *Myth of the Cave*:

I.   514a ("'make an image' of our nature in its education and want of education.")

II.   515c ("consider what their release and healing from bonds and folly would be like…")

III.   516e ("If such a man were to come down again.")

IV.   517a ("this image as a whole must be connected with what was said before.") Let's examine them in greater detail.

V.   Plato asks us to look upon men as though they lived underground; their legs and necks in bonds since childhood. What they see is only that which is in front of them and they cannot turn around to see the source of the light that illuminates their cave. Between the light and the 'prisoners' there is a road and along the road there is a wall. Along this wall men carry objects and utter strange sounds. Those in the cave see these objects as images cast against the wall of their cave.

VI.   The release of the prisoners. "Take a man who is released and suddenly compelled to stand up, to turn his neck around, to walk and look up toward the light."

VII.   If the prisoner who was released were "to come down again" and compete with those still in the cave, "wouldn't he be the source of laughter…"

VIII. Plato calls this turning around, going up and coming back down of the prisoner in the myth the "soul's journey up to the intelligible place."

IX.   In the field of that which can be known "the *idea* of the Good" is that which is seen last and only after considerable effort. But "once seen, it must be concluded that this is in fact the cause of all that is right and fair..."

X.   "The man who is going to act prudently in private or in public must see it."

XI.   For Plato, education is a turning around from perishable things (*ta onta*) to that which is (*to on*) and 'the good' which is "the brightest part of that which is (*tou onta*)." That is "*the good*" (*Agathon*).

The influence of *daimonic* men whose souls are open to the Agathon, men whom Aristotle called *spoudaioi*, mature men, transmit the order of their souls into political order. Plato's allegory reveals this essential truth. Just like the man in the cave "compelled" to "turn around," so the order of the soul enters political community through the attraction to truth of those whose journey took them to that "intelligible place." Later, these ideas resonated with Christian believers who were brought the Gospels through the language of Greek philosophy. Through the discovery of Greek philosophy, the truths of Christianity were transmitted into the modern era.[7]

Though the most influential concept of Aristotle's was his concept of "right by nature" or what today we call "natural law," Enlightenment concepts of "natural rights" dominated the reasoning that justified seeking independence from the British Crown. We return to this dichotomy in Chapter 5 where we examine the contest between ideas implicit in the Declaration of Independence and the Constitution of the United States. But, here, it is of value to re-

---

[7] We examine the importance of this concept in Chapter 11.

view what Aristotle had to say, an understanding that ran counter to
the influence of Progressives made possible by mid-20ᵗʰ-century
classical political theorists who appreciated his arguments.

Aristotle, like Plato, grappled with the argument of the Sophists
that nature and law are opposed, that there are no absolute standards of justice except the ability of the strong to subdue the weak.
Both Plato and Aristotle believed, however, that nature and law are
not opposed, that they are intimately related, and that the Sophistic
argument should not be allowed to stand unchallenged. An equivalent argument is the view commonly held today that what is "right"
depends on the "values" of the particular individual who makes the
valuation. According to this view, nothing is right or wrong absolutely because everyone is different. The sincerity of a person's valuation determines the justice of an ethical judgment, not the nature
of justice.

It is interesting that "nature" was chosen by Plato and Aristotle
to delineate the concept of objective justice by which they refuted
the Sophistic position. They were in search of a concept of that
which is, of reality. And, even today, we speak of "human nature"
or of "nature's course," and we mean something that is structured,
settled, and independent of the will of man. Yet Aristotle's discussion of right by nature, what came in the Latin world to be called *lex
naturalis* and *jus naturale* ("natural law" and "natural right"), suggests
that this understanding is incomplete. It was another aspect of the
meaning of nature (*physis*) that led Aristotle to choose this term.

What is "right by nature,"[8] Aristotle says, does not exist by
people thinking it to be so, but everywhere it must have the same
force. However, some people note that what is recognized as just is
different and changeable and thus assume that all justice is merely
conventional. Aristotle agrees that all justice is changeable, but it
does not follow that all justice is conventional. He says there is
justice by nature and not by convention. But justice by nature is

---

[8] Aristotle, *Nicomachean Ethics*, Martin Ostwald, trans. (Indianapolis:
Bobbs-Merrill, 1962), 1134b6-1135a5.

also changeable. Moreover, Aristotle tells us that it is evident which sort of justice is by nature and which is merely legal and conventional.

We might say, "Well, what is evident to Aristotle is not evident to us." And we might ask, "Who knows?" and "What, after all, is right by nature?" Moreover, "How can it be true, if it changes?" In order to answer these questions, we must refer to what Aristotle says about precision. The degree of precision in the matter of what is right by nature is necessarily a function of finding the measure. We could not be very precise about the weight of an elephant if the measure we used was that commonly used for liquid quantities. The fragile character of right by nature likewise requires a suitable measure and that, he says, is the just man, the *spoudaios*.

Two passages in the *Nicomachean Ethics* define the spoudaios:

> Thus, what is good and pleasant differs with different characteristics or conditions, and perhaps the chief distinction of a man of high moral standards is his ability to see the truth in each particular moral question, since he is, as it were, the standard and measure for such questions.[9]

But in all matters of this sort we consider that to be real and true which appears so to a good man. If this is right, as it seems to be, and if virtue or excellence and the good man, insofar as he is good, are the measure of each thing, then what seem to him to be pleasures are pleasures and what he enjoys is pleasant.[10]

In its realization, or actualization, right by nature is changeable, diverse; yet at the same time, it is unchangeable and everywhere the same, in the sense that what is right in the specific instance of concrete human action will always be seen to be so by the *spoudaios*. The circumstances in which we make ethical judgments are always changing, but what is right will always be judged correctly by the

---

[9] Ibid., 1113a30f.
[10] Ibid., 1176a15.

good man. He possesses the virtue of *phronesis*.

A passage in the *Eudemian Ethics* may explain Aristotle's reasoning. Aristotle asks, "What is the commencement of movement in the soul? The answer is clear, as in the universe, so in the soul, God moves everything."[11] In this we may, perhaps, understand Aristotle's use of the symbol "nature" as a concept applicable to human action, ethics. There is a connection between ethics and ontology, and the ontological symbol of *physis* best reflects that connection.

Where is the connection? The above-mentioned passage gives us a clue. Nature, *physis*, was theophanous, evoking an experience of divine reality which they understood was the *arche*, origin, of nature. From the unmoved mover, the first cause of being, the movement of being flows into the range of human action. Similarly, Plato spoke of the *phronimos* as the man who experienced the *Agathon* and acts with *phronesis*. These concepts express the connection between the movement of being *and* the field of *ethics,* human action. The *daimonic* soul of the *spoudaios* is permeable, open, to the movement of being and is the judge in the changing instances of human action of what is right by nature.

This formulation should be contrasted with the modern notion of "natural rights," with which Aristotle's concept of "right by nature" conflicts in several particulars. What is "right by nature" is not knowable by everyone: it is known only by the mature man. Some men, we infer, will never know what is right by nature because they themselves live lives closed to the divine, that is, fundamentally unjust lives. Aristotle also emphasizes a consciousness of what is right, not the possession of *a* right. It is conceivable, therefore, that the exercise of a "natural right" could conflict with what is right.

For Aristotle, however, right and justice were synonymous. The modern view to the contrary seeks preservation of rights "by any means necessary," that is, even to the exclusion of justice. Thus the

---

[11] Aristotle, *The Works of Aristotle, Vol. IX, Ethica Eudemian*, J. Solomon, trans. (London: Oxford University Press, 1963), 1248a25.

end of government is seen to be the preservation of rights as opposed to justice, order, or the common good. Furthermore, Aristotle's concept of right was linked to his concept of nature, thus giving an ontological association to a basically political concept.

Because nature (*physis*) for the Greek philosophers from Thales to Aristotle was theophanous, Aristotle used the concept of *physis* to evoke an experience of the relationship of law, justice, order, and community with the divine. The modern concept of "natural rights," however, are above politics, fundamentally unlimited, autonomous, both of the political community and of justice. Whereas "right by nature" in Greek philosophy and its Latin formulation, "natural law," were limitations on the state, natural rights have become a chief means by which modern ideologues justify the extension of state power into areas hitherto considered private.

Ancient Rome

We who are participants in Western civilization have been shaped by the experience of ancient Israel, ancient Greece and ancient Rome. Many of the Framers of the Constitution had learned Latin and studied the rise and decline of Rome because they knew that the fall of the Roman Empire, like the new American republic they had fashioned, someday would also experience decline.

Their study of Roman history revealed the aggression of the city of Rome that united the Italian peninsula in the fourth and third centuries BC. Rome then turned to the city of Carthage (contemporary Tunis) and for one hundred and twenty years (between 264 BC and 146 BC), the Romans waged three wars with Carthage. These "Punic Wars" ended with Rome's destruction of Carthage.

Polybius

Polybius (c. 200 BC - c. 118 BC), who lived in this period, attributed Rome's success to a "Mixed Constitution." That constitution sustained three equal powers so carefully balanced that none "could say whether the constitution on the whole were an aristocracy or democracy or despotism."[12] The Consuls, when in Rome and before leaving on military campaigns, held all administrative authority. If there were matters that the populous must approve, the Consuls convened their gathering to make a decision.

The Roman Senate was responsible for finance of infrastructure, and in matters involving crimes and major contests among powerful interests, the Senate decided. In matters of life or death and peace and war, however, the populous decided, not the Senate.[13] Military service was compulsory, and military experience came to be the bond that held the people of Rome in support of those wielding power.[14]

The ancient world in which the Roman empire came to rule the world was changing, and the Consuls of Rome responded to challenges from northern European tribes. That explains why Emperor Hadrian visited Britain in 122 BC and supervised construction of a wall and why Julius Caesar was Governor of Gaul. Ultimately, the pressure of northern tribes overwhelmed Rome's defenses and in 410 AD, Alaric and his Goths invaded Rome.

In Book VI of Polybius's *Histories*, confirmation was found of what the Framers of the Constitution in 1787 already knew from their school days. Of the three types of regimes, kingship, aristocracy, and democracy, the best was a mixture of all three. " ...it is plain that we must regard as the best constitution that which partakes of all these three elements."[15]

Polybius further refined this insight by observing that a kingship is only that regime where rule is accepted voluntarily and "directed by an appeal to reason rather than to fear and force." An ar-

---

[12] *The Histories of Polybius. Book Six*, 357.

[13] Ibid., 358.

[14] Ibid., 361.

[15] *The Histories of Polybius. Book Six.* Evelyn S. Shuckburgh, trans. (Publications Greek Series, Cambridge, Ontario, 2002), 350. http://yorku.ca/inpar/polybius_six.pdf.

istocracy presides where "power is wielded by the justest and wisest men selected on their merits." And a democracy is not a regime where everyone has a right to do "whatever they wish or propose" but where the will of the majority is governed by "reverence to the gods, succor of parents, respect to elders" and "obedience to laws are traditional and habitual."

To the first three regimes, kingship, aristocracy, and democracy must be added "despotism, oligarchy, and mob-rule." And Polybius suggested that there is a "regular cycle" or "natural order" of changes or "revolutions" or regimes from Kingship to Aristocracy to Democracy.[16]

Cicero

For the educated American colonists who looked to Rome for ideas, historical knowledge and legal theory, the works of Marcus Tullius Cicero (106 BC-43 BC) were important aspects of their understanding.

Natural law scholar, Walter Nicgorski, writes that Cicero's thought and very phrases reached to America's founding generations. Thomas Jefferson explicitly names Cicero as one of a handful of major figures who contributed to a tradition 'of public right' that informed his draft of the Declaration of Independence and shaped American understandings of 'the common sense' basis for the right of revolution. Cicero's *On Duties*, highly regarded and influential throughout much of Western history, was regularly present in the libraries of early America. John Adams and James Wilson were notable in the founding period for recalling Cicero and his teaching on 'the principles of nature and eternal reason.'[17] *De Natura Deorum, De Officiis, De Re Publica* and *De Legibus* and Cicero's "disputations" are just a few of Cicero's works that were read by

---

[16] Ibid., 355.

[17] Walter Nicgorski, " Cicero and the Natural Law," The Witherspoon Institute, 2011, http://www.nlnrac.org/classical/cicero

those in colonial America fortunate to have a classical education.

At the College of New Jersey (later named Princeton), John Witherspoon instructed James Madison in the ancient philosophy of Plato and Aristotle. At William and Mary in Virginia, William Small, a scientist and medical doctor, instructed Thomas Jefferson in the works of John Locke, Adam Smith, and David Hume. George Washington, lacking a classical education, sought the instruction of George Mason.

The works of Cicero offered these men a practical philosophy that resolved questions that concerned men of the Enlightenment. Here are some key concepts:

- the importance of piety, reverence, and religion
- man is endowed with reason (*ratio*)
- reason is pervasive in all nature and is divine
- we have innate ideas impressed on us before we were born
- virtue cannot exist without reason and reason exists in man
- there is divine providence
- laws unite human beings with the gods
- the same virtue may be found in man and god
- what is right has been established by nature
- there is right by nature
- law rules the whole cosmos
- there are just wars
- nature's laws govern the affairs of man

Cicero answered questions that the Framers of the Constitution of the United States had about religion, the existence of God, God's Providence, and the distinction between the laws of men and "natural law." The Framers understood that there is "Justice," and that what is "right" is not founded in the will of the powerful, nor is it a matter of opinion.

Christianity

Christianity, which emerged from ancient Israel, reinforces these principles and became a universal religion. In 313 AD, the Emperor Constantine issued the Edict of Milan, which legalized Christianity throughout the Roman Empire. In 380 AD, Emperor Theodosius I went further, issuing the Edict of Thessalonica, which proclaimed Christianity the official religion of the Roman Empire. These decisions preserved the best of ancient Roman and Greek concepts of order while subtly directing that order to conform to the Christian Gospels.

The journey to public acceptance of Christianity, however, was preceded by persecutions. St. Peter and St. Paul both were executed during the reign of Nero (died 85 AD), and Christians were persecuted in public forums. Emperor Diocletion (284 AD) renewed the persecution of Christians and, as we will see, St. Augustine, writing even as late as 410 AD when Goths had invaded Rome, was compelled to defend Christianity from the complaint of Romans that this invasion was a punishment for making Christianity the state religion. Old religions die hard, however, and the gods of the cosmos, what Christians called "pagan" gods, were still held in respect by Romans even though Christianity was the state religion. While this transition from a "pagan" to a Christian order happened long ago, the history of that period is seldom taught in American undergraduate college programs.[18]

Christianity is the faith of believers in the death and resurrection of Jesus Christ. For followers of Jesus, and Jews living in Roman Palestrina when Jesus was alive, the times were rife with predictions of a Messiah. Significantly, Jesus was born in Bethlehem which was prophesied by Micah as the place where a ruler of Israel would be born. Three Magi visited the infant Jesus because they, too, were awaiting the arrival of a new king.

---

[18] See a "Glossary" of key words, persons, and events from the early Christian to the late Medieval era in Appendix A.

The Gospels tell us that, as an adult, Jesus went to visit John the Baptist and the Holy Spirit descended upon Jesus. John baptized Jesus who then retired into the wilderness where Satan attempted to divert him from obedience to God. Jesus worked miracles that amazed his disciples and was even seen walking on the Sea of Galilee. Though Jesus did not encourage claims that he was the long-awaited Messiah, he came into conflict with the Pharisees and the Sadducees, Jewish religious factions of the time. Welcomed by the residents of Jerusalem in what is now celebrated as "Palm Sunday," Jesus was soon thereafter seized and brought before the High Priest of the Sanhedrin—a Jewish Court. Convicted of blasphemy, Jesus was taken to the Roman governor, Pontius Pilate, who allowed a sentence of death.

The crucifixion of Jesus might have been the end of this history, but Jesus rose from the dead and walked with his disciples, taking food with them. Some persons who had not known him in life encountered the risen Christ—St. Paul's encounter on the road to Damascus is one example.[19] Christians believe that they, too, encounter a living Christ. We call those experiences "mystic." Jesus taught that God's kingdom was at hand and preached with urgency that we should follow God's commandments. God's kingdom, however, was not of this world. Many of the first Christians expected Christ to come again very soon and prepared for his Second Coming.

What Christians call the "Old Testament" tells us that God had made a covenant with Israel, but Jesus preached an exacting New Covenant. Christ taught, for example, that we should turn the other cheek and love our enemies, be chaste and avoid temptation, and understand marriage as an insoluble bond. Today, we read the Sermon on the Mount, and Christians recite a prayer that Jesus taught called "The Lord's Prayer." So, too, did masses of peoples of the ancient world who were attracted to the teachings of Jesus.

Jesus' concern for the humble and poor of spirit explains why

---

[19] Galatians 1:11-16.

he attracted believers, but also, Jesus' claim that Christ's kingdom is not of this world became universal. St. Paul, known as "Saul" before his encounter with the resurrected Christ, was instrumental in bringing the Gospel message to non-Jews. Saul, a Roman citizen, was a zealous persecutor of Christians until Christ came to him on the road to Damascus. So powerful was this experience that Saul fell to the ground. A voice speaking in Hebrew said, "Saul, why persecutest thou Me?" Christ explained that he chose him to lead men to be sanctified by faith. Paul then became the Apostle to the Gentiles—non-Jews.

If you are a believing Christian, reading Paul's letters to Christians in Asia Minor will resonate with your own "mystic" experience. But, you do not have to be a Christian to understand our very human love of life and the appeal of the Christian promise of eternal life. That teaching of Christianity was affirmed by the Pharisees who also believed in a last judgment and in a resurrection. Christ's resurrection may be seen as an affirmation of the idea of Greek philosophy that man should aspire to be deathless and teaches us how to live a virtuous life. Try to imagine how these words were heard by the citizens of the cities that St. Paul visited, Corinth, Ephesus, Phillipi, and many others. How does the thought of a Last Judgment and your own personal resurrection affect you?

The early Church preserved the Gospels through "Councils," the first being the Council of Nicaea (325 AD) that affirmed, for an Empire where Christianity had within recent memory been made legal, a common confession. When Christians recite the Nicene Creed, they affirm that God is one, yet three persons; Father, Son, and Holy Spirit. The clarity provided by the Councils enabled the Fathers of the Church to sustain early Christianity through their vigorous "apologetics," or defense of the faith. The most influential of the Fathers of the Church is St. Augustine, Bishop of Hippo. Hippo is a port city in what today is known as Annaba in Algeria.

St. Augustine's massive *City of God* is a defense of Christians against Romans who blamed them for the fall of Rome and a critical work that defines the limits of state power. Augustine writes about:

- His sinful life before conversion to Christianity;
- His attraction to the Manichean religion;
- The City of God—a community of all persons who love God;
- The City of Man—the material world governed by appetite and dominated by lust for domination;
- Original Sin—the desire to make man the center of the universe;
- The "elect"—those saved by God, thus recognizing that not all will be saved;
- The state—has a place—a necessary evil—in sustaining social order but is not the way to salvation;
- Progress—the way to salvation taken by faithful Pilgrims; progress is spiritual not material; and
- Evil—turning away from God.

By the end of the 5th century AD, "barbarian" tribes ruled all of Italy, but as Rome was felled by invaders, there rose the successors to St. Peter, Bishops of Rome, who eked out a spiritual space independent from invading tribes and, ultimately, converted the invaders to Christianity. Two of these early Bishops were Gelasius I and Gregory the Great. This conversion to Christianity of the invading tribes affirmed a moral order that has ever been the hallmark of Western civilization. The continuity of that order from classical antiquity to what is called the Middle Ages was maintained by the Church.

"First Europe" and the Middle Ages

The new Christian civilization that developed from the fall of

Rome in 5th century AD to the 10th century is called "First Europe." In order to understand the humble, barren, violent, and desperate lives of men and women who lived in Europe during that period, we need only comprehend what historians tell us. What we learn is that we ourselves would not want to have lived in those times.

Sixth-century Italian culture, writes the American medieval historian Norman Cantor, "was marked by the decline of cities and literary, the progressive ruralization of the economy, and the advance of ignorance and superstition."[20] In the year 800 AD, during the reign of Charlemagne, half of Europe was covered by dense forests. Society was based around castles, churches, and monasteries, but a castle was a mere wooden stockade, and churches were erected in stone that were low, squat and reminiscent of Roman bathhouses.[21] Scholars coming to this study today will find men and women with whom we can identify. Norman Cantor, writes, "The vitality and boldness of the intellectual leaders of the twelfth century could scarcely be surpassed."[22]

Who were these men and women of First Europe? What struggles did they confront? What did they attempt to achieve and what became of their achievement? This listing of 11th- and 12th-century "Greats" is instructive:

- Pope Gregory VII (1015-1085) who initiated the Investiture Controversy;
- Hugh the Great (1024-1109), Abbot at Cluny;
- St. Anselm (1033-1109), Archbishop of Canterbury;
- Pope Paschal II (c. 1050-1118), last of four Gregorian "reformers;"
- Henry IV (1050-1106), excommunicated three times by

---

[20] Norman F. Cantor, *The Civilization of the Middle Ages; Medieval History-The Life and Death of a Civilization* (New York: Harper Collins, 1993), 157.

[21] Ibid., 187.

[22] Ibid., 203.

Pope Gregory VII;

- Peter Abelard (1079-1142) and the love of his life,
- Heloise (1090-1164);
- St. Bernard of Clairvaux (1090-1153);
- John of Salisbury (1120-1180);
- Frederick I of Germany (1122-1190);
- Richard the Lion-heart (1157-1199); and
- Philip II Augustus of France (1165-1223).

These great "First Europeans," and their predecessors, established a political order in which it was possible for St. Thomas Aquinas, Albertus Magnus, Siger de Brabant, Marsilius of Padua, William of Ockham, and others in the 13th century to engage in philosophical and theological discourses that interpreted the civilization and culture of the West as national monarchies came into dominance.

It took five centuries, from the invasion of Rome in 410 AD by Visigoths led by Alaric (c. 470-410 AD), to shape the intellectual basis of a new civilization. The culture of that civilization became what we call "Christendom," and the history of that period shaped what is called "First Europe." Once order had been stabilized, a new, vibrant, civilization developed that shaped the West during what we call the "Middle Ages."

Even by the 13th century, as life became better, the lives of our predecessors were much less comfortable than our own. City life was characterized by bad housing, bad sanitation, overcrowding, destructive fires, and drunken violence.[23] Over twenty years, in the 14th century, plague in the form of the "Black Death" killed one third of the population in Europe.[24]

This then-new and vibrant civilization is visible in a cacophony of royal dynasties, the institution of new modes of spiritual life in

---

[23] Ibid., 476.
[24] Ibid., 481.

"monasticism," the assertion of dominion of the Roman Church and its Papacy, and the many saints, philosophers, Crusades, major battles, heresies, and millennial movements that we associate with Christian civilization during First Europe.

We can begin to see what this entailed in this brief, but complex, schema:

Monastic Orders: Eremites, Benedictine, Cluniac, Dominican, Franciscan, Cistercian, Carthusian

Popes: Gregory I, Gregory II, Leo III, Sylvester II, Leo IX, Paschal II, Gregory VII, Urban II, Calixtus VII, Adrian IV

Church Councils:

Nicaea (325 AD), adopted the Nicene Creed
Second Council of Nicaea (787), repudiated Iconoclasm
First Lateran Council (1123), investiture of Bishops
Second Lateran Council (1139), addressed clerical discipline
Third Lateran Council (1179), restricted election of Popes to Cardinals
Fourth Lateran Council (1214), established seven Sacraments

Saints: Boniface, Benedict, Denis, Anselm, Bernard, Thomas, Francis, Bonaventure, Dominic

Philosophers: Thomas Aquinas, Averroes, Siger de Brabant, Roger Bacon, William of Ockham, Duns Scotus, Maimonides, Avicenna

Heresies: Joachite, Albigensian, Donatist, Gnostic

Millennial Movements: The Pasteraux, Drummer of Niklashausen

Crusades: First (1095), Second (1144), Third (1190), Fourth (1204),

Anti-Albigensian (1209)

Major Battles: Civitate (1053), Hastings (1066), Manzikert (1071), Legnano (1174), Las Navas de Tolosa (1212), Muret (1213), Bouvines (1214)

Dynasties: Merovingian, Capetian, Angevin, Carolingian

Monarchs: Philip I, William the Conqueror, Henry IV, Philip II, Frederick I Barbarossa, Richard the Lion Heart

There is much to digest in this schema, but these last two entries, the succession of monarchs and dynasties, are central to our examination of the contest between Western man's consciousness of what is just and the necessities of political rule. By the actions of monarchs of this era, we can track the development of the order of nations, their politics, and the royal and noble persons who contested with the papacy and shaped a new political culture.

Study of this "Medieval" history reveals persons and personalities who are exciting to us because they offer a point of reference similar to our own, though we were born more than one thousand years later. The world of nation-states that we have inherited from them was shaped by contests with these monarchs:

Philip I (c. 1052 –July 29, 1108) became monarch in 1060 on the death of Henry I and occupied the throne for the next forty-eight years.[25] Philip I was a descendent of Hugh Capet who in 987 was preferred by the Archbishop of Rouen over Duke Charles of Lorraine to succeed Louis V who had no legitimate offspring. The Capetian monarchy ruled France until 1328.

Philip II Augustus of France (1165-1223), whose victory at

---

[25] John Julius Norwich, *A History of France* (New York: Atlantic Monthly Press, 2018), 18.

the Battle of Bouvines in Flanders in 1214 shaped the order of Europe literally to the present time.

William the Conqueror (1028-1087), whose conquest of England established the great English monarchy. The "Normans" who carried out the "Norman Conquest" were Bretons from Normandy in northwest France, themselves descendants of Norse "Vikings" from Denmark, Norway, and Iceland.

Henry IV (1056-1106) and Frederick I Barbarossa of Germany (1122-1190) who challenged the assertions of the papacy.

These early monarchies became centers of political order of civilization in the West.

The great question asked here is whether Christendom, embodied in our consciousness of the philosophical and theological experience of the West from ancient Israel to the Christian Gospels, continues to shape the nations and culture of the West today and, if not, does that loss of consciousness contribute to the fragility and very survival of civilization in the West and democracy in America? How deep is the decline of this "Post-Christian" era in which we live? Where, then, do we begin?

Dates are significant, but only as references to events, important actions of men and women, and their motives. Behind historical events, the spirit and motives of the main actors are most important. Clearly, the greatest motivation that shaped the West after the fall of the Roman Empire was Christian faith. That faith took form and had its greatest influence in Christian monasticism.

Monasticism

Celtic (5th century AD)

Celtic Christians exhibited forms of monasticism at Iona, Lindisfarne, and Kildare. St. Columban (543-615) advocated a monastic rule that included confession of sins and penitential acts.

Benedictine (5th century AD)

St. Benedict of Nursia (480-c. 547), formulated the "Rule of St. Benedict" used by Benedictines for fifteen centuries, and is considered the founder of Western Christian monasticism. Originally a hermit, St. Benedict came to understand the limits and dangers of eremetic hermeticism and fashioned a standard of community living, the "Rule of St. Benedict," that prescribed how to live a life in community, cenobitic hermeticism, with other monks committed to poverty, celibacy, and work that supported the community. Gregory I, Pope in 590, employed the Benedictine monks, led by Augustine of Canterbury, as missionaries to England.

St. Boniface (675-754), engaged in the conversion of German tribes to Christianity, imposed the rule of St. Benedict, and built monasteries that became vital centers of German monastic life.

Cluniac (910)

The early monastic orders identified with the Burgundian monastery of Cluny, founded in 910 AD. Cluny was the largest, best endowed, and most prestigious, devoted to the perpetuation of the Benedictine form of discipline. The monastery at Cluny flourished because it was immune from lay and episcopal interference and supported the principle of theocratic kingship. The monastery was led by Abbot Hugh of Cluny (d. 1109), whose good judgment may be seen in the fact that he detested the aggressive puritanism of Pope Gregory VII (1015-1085).

Carthusian (1084)

Founded by St. Bruno who introduced a Rule, called the *Statutes,* that prescribed how a Carthusian hermit life, based in solitude, was to be lived.

Cistercian (1098)

An order of ascetics founded by the Englishman, Stephen Harding

(1060-1134), in Citeaux in eastern France. St. Bernard of Clairvaux joined the monastery in 1112, and the order expanded throughout Western Europe in the 12th century. The Cistercians sought a return to the literal observance of the Rule of St. Benedict.

Eremetic Monasticism (11th century AD)

By the middle of the 11th century, lay piety became socially important and desire for personal religious experience took the form of eremetic monasticism. Peter Damian (c. 1007-c. 1072), Cardinal and Benedictine monk, was an eremetic who engaged in reform of clergy in northern Italy and introduced more severe monastic disciplines including flagellation. Damian denounced the corruption of the secular clergy and sought to purify the clergy in anticipation of the Second Coming that he believed was imminent.

Franciscan (1209)

Founded by St. Francis Assisi (1181-1226), son of a wealthy merchant, St. Francis devoted himself to a life of poverty. He composed the *Regula primitiva* or "Primitive Rule" submitted to Pope Innocent III in 1209. The Primitive Rule called followers "to live in obedience, in chastity and without anything of their own and to follow the teaching and the footprints of our Lord Jesus Christ..."[26]

Dominican (1216)

Founded by Dominic of Caleruega in France, and approved by Pope Honorius III in 1216, to preach the Gospel and to oppose heresy. Known as the Order of Preachers, the Dominican order came to dominate the cathedral school in Paris and is identified by the most important philosopher of the Church, the Dominican saint, Thomas Aquinas.

In addition to these monastic orders that attracted the "best and

---

[26] https://ofm.org/en/the-rule.html

brightest," there were the Popes.

Popes

The first great monarchies of First Europe were supported by a doctrine of theocratic kingship and the Petrine doctrine of primacy of St. Peter through whom Christ established his Church. A succession of Bishops of Rome, as head of the Church, shaped Christian doctrine and struggled to assert the power of the Papacy over Christian monarchs.

Gelasius I (d.496), was the author of *Tractatus IV* and *Epistula XII* (492 and 496) who developed the principle of separation of spiritual and temporal powers, distinguishing between *auctoritas sacrata pontificum*, papal authority, and *regalis potestas*, royal power.[27]

Gregory I (540-604), known as St. Gregory the Great, commissioned a mission to convert the Anglo-Saxons of England,

Gregory II (669-731), commissioned Boniface to preach to the Germans.

Gregory III (d.741), requested from Charles Martel protection of "the church of St. Peter" and gave formal expression to the reality of a secular power.

Leo III (d. 816), crowned Charlemagne Holy Roman Emperor. Eric Voegelin writes, "With the coronation of Charlemagne the idea of the empire had been created that was to dominate the centuries of medieval political history."[28]

---

[27] Eric Voegelin, *The Middle Ages to Aquinas, The Collected Works, Vol. 20*, Peter von Sivers ed. (Columbia, MO: University of Missouri Press, 1997), 53.

[28] Ibid., 59.

Sylvester II (946-1003), Gerbert of Aurillac, a renowned scholar and counselor to Otto III.

Leo IX (1002-1054), appointed Pope by Emperor Henry III, but sought election in Rome.

Paschal II (1050-1118), a monk of the Cluniac order. Contested claims of King Henry V of Germany (1081-1125) and ceded to the King's investiture as Emperor.

Pope Gregory VII (1015-1085), led an attempt to carry his ascetic interests to the whole church and create a unified Christian world, what Gregory VII called a *Christianitas*. He became Pope in 1073, and precipitated the "Investiture Controversy" that attempted to deny the right of kings and great lords to invest bishops and abbots with the symbols of their office.

In asserting that principle, he demanded that Henry IV, Emperor of the Germans, give up his claim to lay investiture. When Henry refused, Gregory VII excommunicated the emperor and deposed him. That act shook the foundations of feudal society and compelled King Henry to seek forgiveness. In an historic meeting, King Henry IV and Gregory VII met in 1077 at the castle of Canossa, in northern Italy where Gregory was required by tradition and law to grant absolution to a penitent and confessed sinner. Abbot Hugh of Cluny (who detested Pope Gregory) appeared in person to intercede on Henry's behalf.

Pope Gregory's assertion of papal power was a high water mark in the contest between monarchies that would come to dominate Western Europe and ultimately the waning earthly powers of the papacy. Henry IV retaliated eight years later in 1085 by invading Italy and driving Gregory VII from Rome.

Philosophers

The philosophers of this era, are also important. They shaped the intellectual culture of the West and even the self-understanding of monarchs and popes. But man does not live by ideas alone, and the nation-states prevailed over the philosophers and the Papacy thus establishing a contest between conscience and political power.

In the works of the early and late philosophers of First Europe, we can see the consequences of political ideas, from St. Augustine through Gelasius, St. John of Salisbury, and St. Thomas, men who were not merely "thinkers," but who also evoked our consciousness of order and participation in divine reality with their whole personalities. When they engaged in those actions (for to think is to "act"), the times in which they lived were given new importance.

Americans who lived through more than 60 years of "World Wars" in the 20th century will appreciate that from 1214-1290, the 13th century benefited from seventy-six years of peace. During that time, Europe experienced an outburst of artistic, cultural, and philosophical accomplishment. That was made possible by the work of four intellectuals who lived from 1033 to 1180: St. Anselm, Roscelin, Peter Abelard, and John of Salisbury.

St. Anselm (1033-1109) was a Benedictine and Archbishop of Canterbury, St. Anselm was exiled by William II (the Conqueror) and Henry I for defending the Papacy during Gregory VII's dispute over the power of Investiture.

St. Anselm's *Proslogium* attempts to prove the existence of God though it appears not to be in response to anyone who denied God's existence. In other words, St. Anselm valued thinking in itself and by giving a "proof" of God's existence was affirming his love of God. The problem with that is that God is not a "thing," the existence of which can be proven. Chapter XIV of the *Proslogium* touches on the motivation for his inquiry.

"... if you have found him, why is it that you do not feel you have found him? Why, O Lord, our God, does not my soul feel you, if it has found you?"

Here Anselm asks a question more important than whether God exists. "Why do I doubt?" In other words, my own lack of faith is a problem. How can I resolve that?

Finally, in Chapter XXV, Anselm answers his question: "Why, then, do you wander abroad, slight man, in your search for the goods of your soul and your body? Love the one good in which are all goods, and it suffices."

Roscelin of Compiègne (1050-1125) was a "Nominalist" and held that what we know are words, not the things themselves.

Peter Abelard (1070-1142) began as a student of Roscelinus and entered the Cathedral School at Paris where he attracted the enmity of his teacher. Abelard, like modern scholars, was not one to remain silent, a condition that he endured for scholarly and personal reasons. His affair with Heloise, the birth of their illegitimate son, a violent and abusive attack on his physical person, and his career as a wandering lecturer inform our appreciation of the hardships and attractions of life in the 12th century.

Peter Abelard's "*Sic et Non*" is a list of propositions and counter propositions that left unanswered which was truth and which was falsehood. These questions that have occupied faithful Christians for centuries, opened Abelard to criticism, though he seemed to delight in controversy.

1. Must human faith be completed by reason, or not?
2. Does faith deal only with unseen things, or not?
3. Is there any knowledge of things unseen, or not?
4. May one believe only in God alone, or not?
5. Is God a single unitary being, or not?
6. Is God divided into three parts, or not?
7. Is God to be seen as a part of everything, as present in everything, or not?

8. Does the first Psalm speak about the Messiah, or not?
9. Does God's foreknowledge determine outcomes, or not?
10. Does anything happen by accident or coincidence, or not?
11. Can even sins please God, or not?
12. Is God the cause and initiator of evil, or not?
13. Can God do anything and everything, or not?
14. Is it possible to resist God, or not?
15. Does God have free will, or not?
16. Does God do whatever He wants, or not?
17. Does anything happen contrary to God's will, or not?
18. Does God know everything, or not?[29]

John of Salisbury (1120-1180) was secretary to the English Pope Adrian IV before returning to England in 1153 to became secretary to the Archbishop of Canterbury, Theobald of Bec (1090-1161). He was a close associate of Thomas Beckett (b. 1119), Archbishop of Canterbury from 1162 until his murder in 1170 at the hands of supporters of English king, Henry II. Beckett's murder reveals the intensity of the conflict between conscience and power.

John of Salisbury's *Policraticus* was written before the introduction of the works of Aristotle, yet it is a treatise on politics that deals realistically with the issue of power. Like St. Augustine, John of Salisbury distinguishes between persons who love themselves (*amor sui*) and those who love God (*amor Dei*), but John of Salisbury uses those concepts not as aspects of a history of salvation but as empirical descriptions of men in the world. He is especially descriptive of the *amor sui* of personalities that are normal within what he calls *vita politicorum* or the political state.[30] Constrained by the concepts at hand, he describes political reality, without the spirit of a St. Augustine, as tending toward evil.

In light of that perception, John of Salisbury informs our ap-

---

[29]   https://vanaprats.weebly.com/uploads/9/2/1/5/9215274/sic-et-non.pdf

[30] Op. cit., 114-115.

preciation of the contest between conscience and power when he writes that he accepts the power of kings, but not if they resist and oppose the divine commandments.

> "...not only do I submit to his power patiently, but with pleasure so long as it is exercised in subjection to God and follows His ordinances. But on the other hand if (power) resists and opposes the divine commandments, and wishes to make me share in its war against God; then with unrestrained voice I answer back that God must be preferred before any man on earth."[31]

In order to fully appreciate the following century's abundance of intellect and a developing secular order that defines our age, consider the following:

Roger Bacon (1219-1292) wrote the *Compendium Studii Philosophiae,* a rigorous diatribe against the condition of intellectual culture in the 13th century. Revealing is his criticism of "...the prelates; how they run after money, neglect the cure of souls, promote their nephews, and other carnal friends, and crafty lawyers who ruin all by their counsels; for they despise students in philosophy and theology."[32]

> "The whole clergy is intent upon pride, lechery, and avarice; and wherever clerks are gathered together, as at Paris and Oxford, they scandalize the whole laity with their wars and quarrels and other vices."

Of "Doctors of Divinity," he complains " there has never been so

---

[31] Quoted from Chapter XXV of *The Statesman's Book of John of Salisbury*. Translated by John Dickinson. (New York: Alfred A. Knopf, 1927), 258-263, by Fordham University Medieval Sourcebook https://www.sourcebooks.fordham.edu/source/salisbury-poli6-24.asp

[32] From C.G. Coulton, ed., *Life in the Middle Ages* (New York: Macmillan, c. 1910), Vol 2, 55-62 at Fordham University Medieval Sourcebook https://sourcebooks.fordham.edu/source/bacon1.asp

great ignorance." Against university lecturers, he argues that they "have never learned anything of any account." And, he complains, though they become Masters of Theology, they have not learned Greek or Hebrew.

Siger de Brabant (1240-1284) was a contemporary of St. Thomas, and also a prolific writer. Among his works were dissertations including *Impossibilia, Quaestiones logicales, Sophismata,* and commentaries on Aristotle's *De Anima, Physics, Metaphysics* and Treatises, *De Necessitate et contingentia causarum, De aeternitate mundi,* and *De anima intellectiva.*

Because Aristotle's *Physics* and *Metaphysics* were seen as incompatible with Christian doctrine, they were prohibited at the school in Paris in 1210. That prohibition was renewed in 1215 and again in 1263. Aristotle was reintroduced by Albertus Magnus, St. Thomas and William of Moerbeke, however, after 1240.[33]

Siger may be credited for introducing Aristotle through the Commentaries of Averroes. Averroes (1126–1198), in Arabic, ibn Rushd, was an Islamic philosopher born in Cordoba (Spain) who dealt with the problem of the conflict between reason and faith. While believed to have held a theory of "double truth" in which some things were true by reason, others by religion, Averroes demonstrated the contrary in *On the Harmony of Religion with Philosophy,* where he explained:

"Now since this religion is true and summons to the study which leads to knowledge of the Truth, we the Muslim community know definitely that demonstrative study does not lead to [conclusions] conflicting with what Scripture has given us; for truth does not oppose truth but accords with it and bears witness to it."[34]

---

[33] Op. Cit, 179.
[34] George F. Hourani, *Averroes: On the Harmony of Religion and Philosophy* (Edinburgh: Edinburgh University Press, 2007), 22.

Unlike in Christianity, in which reason and faith were reconciled by the Christian scholastics, in Islam, philosophy was, Muslim theologian Al-Ghazali (1058-1111) charged in his *Incoherence of the Philosophers* based on his reading of the works of Al-Farabi (870-950) and Ibn Sina (980-1037), a mode of contemplation for an intellectual elite for whom "belief" in the literal word of the Koran was not sufficient. Commentaries on Aristotle had been, therefore, seen as suspect, "books" evoking an esoteric religion, often irreligious, and sometimes (for instance, in Al-Farabi's and Ibn Sina's avowed disbelief in the resurrection of the body) downright heretical.

Siger's introduction, then, of Aristotle for the purpose of synthesizing faith and reason brought upon him by association with Averroes' works (among which was a bold refutation of Al-Ghazali entitled *The Incoherence of the Incoherence*) a charge of supporting the purported "double truth" theory, and he and his works were condemned in France in 1277 (along with some of the works of St. Thomas Aquinas) by the Parisian Bishop Étienne (Stephen) Tempier (d. 1279). Siger was allegedly murdered in 1284 in Italy where he had fled following his condemnation. Even today, a tendency to make political philosophy a substitute for religious faith, by way of arguing that truth in one sphere is equal to truth in another, is a temptation that seduces many.

St. Thomas Aquinas (1225-1274) was born in the village of Roccasecca, about five miles from the town of Aquino, Italy, the young Thomas was placed at an early age in the monastery of Monte Cassino. In 1239, at the age of 14, he was sent to the University of Naples where he decided to become a Dominican friar. In 1245, he went to Paris where he attended lectures by Albertus Magnus and Roger Bacon. At the University of Paris, he studied the works of Aristotle.

Four years later in 1249 Thomas went to Cologne with Albertus Magnus, and in 1252 he returned to Paris where in 1256, at the age of 31, he earned the Master of Theology. In 1259, he was a lecturer and counselor to the Papal Curia in Rome. From 1265-1267, he lectured in Rome, and in 1268 he was sent to Paris.

At the time that St. Thomas came to maturity, a hundred and seventy five years after the Investiture Controversy created by Pope Gregory VII in 1075, the great nation states of the West were in the early stages of development, and the authority of the Papacy was diminished. Eric Voegelin notes that St. Thomas's *Summa Theologiae* does not address the institution of the Church nor of Canon law. He writes, "Thomas stands between the ages: the medieval unit of imperial Christianity is dead, the world of the national states is not yet born."[35]

The works of Thomas Aquinas include disputations, philosophical commentaries, systematic works (the *Summa Theologiae* and *Summa contra Gentiles*), commentaries on books of the Bible and Liturgical works, letters and Tractates. Dead at age 49, St. Thomas literally worked himself to death.

St. Thomas is important because he is the link itself between faith and reason, between the revelation provided in the Gospels and the discoveries of ancient Greek philosophy coming back into Europe translated into Latin from the Arabic, a language that preserved it for four hundred years as it snaked its way around central Asia and the Middle East, across North Africa and into Spain.

In short, St. Thomas' work gave intellectual understanding to revelation. Though the West's Christian origins have been negated by Enlightenment ideas and the consequences of totalitarian movements, a vibrant faith in Christ and our obligation to our fellow man shines through the destruction those "rational" ideas and "ideologies" caused.

Johan Huizenga in 1919 wrote about the "waning" of the Middle Ages. The title of our study on conscience and power is more

---

[35] Our analysis follows Eric Voegelin, *Collected Works of Eric Voegelin, Vol. 20, History of Ideas* (Columbia, MO: Univ. of Missouri Press, 1998), 207-32. https://voegelinview.com/saint-thomas-aquinas-history-politics-law-part-1

specific: the "waning" of Christianity in the 21st century. That question was asked by a contemporary, a novelist, the late Tom Wolfe (1930-2018), when he observed, on several public occasions, that loss of faith in Christianity has cultural consequences.

We 21st-century Americans have enjoyed a life of great freedom and the benefits of a powerful country that, at its moment of victory in World War II, experienced the consequences of its decline. The many wars of the 20th century brought destruction of political regimes *and* the occlusion of experience of God's presence in the life of participants in the culture of the West. That has made recovery of the philosophical and theological principles of Western civilization extremely difficult.

Our religions and their clergy have been corrupted. Our universities are dominated by ideologues and our legal classes have absorbed "Progressive" notions and have abandoned the philosophy of limited government put forward by the Framers of the Constitution. Moreover, we no longer ask the important questions. Our desire to recover those important questions and the light they shed on political order requires, Voegelin suggests, a fundamental reconstruction of regime analysis by means of the introduction of new concepts.

We begin to see the significance, therefore, of St. Thomas' struggles against the monastic orders that disdained knowledge and intellectual inquiry. St. Thomas had to overcome powerful social forces that disdained the works of Aristotle and in doing so reconciled reason with Christian Revelation. Voegelin writes:

"He had a monumentally ordering mind, and he could apply this mind to a wealth of materials drawn into its orbit by a personality equally distinguished by sensorial receptivity, range of soul, intellectual energy, and sublimeness of spirit."[36]

In *Contra Gentiles*, written to provide intellectual support for

---

[36] Ibid., p. 207.

Dominican missions in Muslim Spain, St. Thomas observes that in refutation of errors with Muslims and pagans, "We must ... have recourse to the natural reason, to which all men are forced to give their assent." Reason leads to the judgment that "There must therefore be some being by whose providence the world is governed."[37] And that "first author and mover of the universe is an intellect."[38] The end of intellect is truth; thus, all men may "easily be able to have a share in the knowledge of God, and this without uncertainty and error."[39] That was not an assumption made by Plato or Aristotle. That link is not perfect.

The ancient Greek philosophers were men for whom humanity was not universal. Plato observes in the *Republic*, for example, that when at war with barbarians Greeks treat them differently than when at war with Greeks who are "by nature friends."[40] Christianity shattered that limited view with an understanding of our common humanity, shaped by the Gospels, based on the universality of mankind.

That consciousness of justice compels all men to deal with all other men as human beings *qua* human. The consequences of this consciousness of the universality of mankind cannot be overstated for our appreciation of the importance of justice. Our "conscience" has been a part of Western culture ever since as it participated in the rise of the West from the ashes of the Roman Empire. Eric Voegelin observes:

"The common man is ... not left without knowledge. What the philosopher knows through the activity of his intellect, the layman knows through the revelation of God in Christ. The supranatural manifestation of the Truth in Christ and its natural

---

[37] *Contra Gentiles, Book One: God,* Anton C. Pegis trans. Online at https://genius.com/St-thomas-aquinas-summa-contra-gentiles-book-i-annotated

[38] Book One, par. 2.

[39] Book One, chapter 4, par. 6.

[40] *Republic,* Book V, 470c.

manifestation in the intellectual as the mature man stand side by side."[41]

Not only has St. Thomas understood that reason is a universal capacity of all men, he carves out a place in Western consciousness for *both* philosophy and revelation. Voegelin frames St. Thomas' achievement in terms of its compatibility of reason with Revelation: "The authority of the intellect is preserved, but through its transcendental orientation it is transformed from an intramundane rival of the faith into a legitimate expression of natural man."[42] He adds that St. Thomas's spirituality "recognizes revelation and cannot conceive of a conflict between natural reason and spirit."[43] This insight is carried over into St. Thomas concept of eternal law, *lex aeterna*, that is an endowment of man's nature, the reality of which is visible in *lex naturalis*, natural law. "The natural law," Aquinas wrote, "is promulgated by the very fact that God instilled it into man's mind so as to be known by him naturally."[44]

John Kilkullen, Professor of History at Macquarie University in Australia, writes that for St. Thomas Aquinas natural law is from the reasonable will of God (q.97 a.3); God's reason, will, and law are identical with God himself (q.93 a.4 ad 1). The ultimate end to which reason directs action is the well-being of the whole community, the common good; every law, therefore, is ordered to the common good (q.90 a.2), and every law is ordered to friendship among those who share this common good (q.99 a.1 ad 2; a.2); the natural law fosters the friendship of all mankind with God. Laws are made and promulgated by someone who has charge of the community. The natural law is promulgated by God's inserting into the

---

[41] Voegelin, *Collected Works of Eric Voegelin, Vol. 20, History of Ideas*, 209.

[42] Ibid., 210.

[43] Ibid.

[44] St. Thomas Aquinas, *The Summa Theologica* (Benziger Bros., 1947), trans. Fathers of the English Dominican Province, 90.4. https://aquinas101.thomisticinstitute.org/st-iaiiae-q-90

minds of human beings a natural capacity to come to know the natural law (q.90 a.4ad 1).[45]

For St. Thomas, there are four aspects of law: eternal, natural, human, and divine. He explains, "the rule and measure of human acts is the reason (ratio), which is the first principle of human acts."[46] Because St. Thomas was not interested in the *polis* of the Greek city-states, he literally "bent" Aristotle to conform to the Christian experience. That entailed a concept of the king as a ruler of free persons.

Aristotle's concept of "slaves by nature" "had no place in a Christian polity." St. Thomas makes freedom or servitude the criterion of good or bad government. "If the members of the community cooperate freely in the enterprise of common existence, the government is good, be it a monarchy, aristocracy, or polity."[47] Man for Aristotle was *zoon politikon*, a political or social animal. But, for St. Thomas man was *homo Christianus* whose life is oriented not merely to the social order of this world, but toward a transcendent end, beyond the world, in life eternal.

Marsilius of Padua (1275-1342) was the author of *Defensor pacis* (1324)[48] and served as Rector of the University of Paris in 1313. He engaged, like William of Ockham, in a dispute with Pope John XXII who asserted the primacy of papal authority over Ludwig of Bavaria. Among Marsilius' provocative conclusions found in his *Defensor pacis* are:

2.   The general council of Christians or its majority alone has

---

[45] John Kilcullen, "Medieval Theories of Natural Rights," published online by Marquarie University Department of Modern History: https://researchers.mq.edu.au/en/publications/natural-rights

[46] St. Thomas Aquinas, *The Summa Theologica*, 90.1.

[47] Voegelin, *Collected Works of Eric Voegelin, Vol. 20, History of Ideas*, 219.

[48] Ephraim Emerton, *Defencor Pacis of Marsiglio of Padua: A Critical Study* (Cambridge, Harvard University Press, 1920). https://archive.org/details/defensorpacisofm08emer/page/n5

the authority to define doubtful passages of the divine law, and to determine those that are to be regarded as articles of the Christian faith, belief in which is essential to salvation; and no partial council or single person of any position has the authority to decide these questions.[49]

3. The gospels teach that no temporal punishment or penalty should be used to compel observance of divine commandments.

7. Decretals and decrees of the bishop of Rome, or of any other bishops or body of bishops, have no power to coerce anyone by secular penalties or punishments, except by the authorization of the human "legislator."

11. There can be only one supreme ruling power in a state or kingdom.

14. No bishop or priest has coercive authority or jurisdiction over any layman or clergyman, even if he is a heretic.

17. All bishops derive their authority in equal measure immediately from Christ, and it cannot be proved from the divine law that one bishop should be over or under another, in temporal or spiritual matters.

22. The prince who rules by the authority of the laws of Christians has the right to determine the number of churches and temples, and the number of priests, deacons, and other clergy who shall serve in them.

39. The people as a community and as individuals, according to their several means, are required by divine law to support the bishops and other clergy authorized by the gospel, so that they may have food and clothing and the other necessaries of life; but the people are not required to pay tithes or other taxes beyond the amount necessary for such support.

---

[49] Oliver J. Thatcher, and Edgar Holmes McNeal, eds., *A Source Book for Medieval History* (New York: Scribners, 1905), 317-324. https://sourcebooks.fordham.edu/source/marsiglio1.asp

John Duns Scotus (1266-1308) wrote *On God as First Principle*,[50] *On Immaculate Conception*, the metaphysics and logic of Aristotle, *Quaestiones super universalia Porphyrii*, and literally dozens of other disquisitions. His treatise *On God as First Principle* is an example of what we call "Scholasticism," or the method of the "schools" of his day, in which analysis used dialectic, or propositional, reasoning. Here is a typical example.

"2.9 (Fourth conclusion) What is not ordered to an end is not an effect.

2.10 The first proof is this. There is no effect which does not stem from some proper efficient cause; if something is not ordered to an end, it does not originate with a proper efficient cause."[51]

His Oxford Lectures, Book III, dealt with a series of questions:

- Whether Christ was predestined to be Son of God?
- Whether the Blessed Virgin was conceived in Original Sin?
- Whether the Blessed Virgin was truly Mother of God and Man? Whether there are in Christ two real filiations?
- Whether between the Blessed Virgin and St. Joseph there was true matrimony?

William of Ockham (1287-1347) was an English Franciscan born in Ockham, a village in Surrey about twenty-five miles from London. A listing of Ockham's works and a brief, but comprehensive, review of his philosophy may be found in the Stanford Encyclopedia of Philosophy.[52]

William of Ockham is known principally as a "nominalist,"

---

[50] https://www.franciscan-archive.org/scotus
[51] https://www.ewtn.com/library/THEOLOGY/GODASFIR.HTM
[52] https://plato.stanford.edu/entries/ockham/#2

which is explained in the Stanford Encyclopedia as follows: "For Ockham, the only universal entities it makes sense to talk about are universal concepts, and derivative on them, universal terms in spoken and written language. Metaphysically, these 'universal' concepts are singular entities like all others; they are 'universal' only in the sense of being 'predicable of many.'"[53]

In short, we are not capable of knowing entities that are universal; what we know are merely names. That does not mean that what is universal does not exist. They are not things in the world of things and cannot be known by sense experience.

Ockham rejected the intrusions of Pope John XXII into the rules of the Franciscans and composed an argument to refute him in his *Dialogus*. The threat of conviction for heresy was real, and having opposed the Pope, Ockham sought protection from King Ludwig of Bavaria, whom Pope John XXII had deposed. Ockham lived in exile in Munich where he died in 1347.

There in *Dialogus* he presents the claims of canonists:

"They say that canonists have the power to examine not only with what penalty according to canon law it is proper to punish heretics, but also how judicial proceedings should be taken against them—that is, how writs of accusation and other writs should be composed, how witnesses should be produced, and other things that pertain to the order of legal proceedings."[54]

Ockham responds in his *Dialogus* by asserting the supremacy of theology over canon law.

"...which assertion is to be regarded as catholic, which as heretical, pertains chiefly to those who treat of the science in which

---

[53] Ibid., 4.2 "The Rejection of Universals."

[54] William of Ockham, *Dialogus*, part 1, prologue and book 1, John Kilcullen and John Scott, trans. (The British Academy, 2003). https://britac.ac.uk/pubs/dialogus/t1d1.html

the rule of orthodox faith is explicitly and completely handed down . Such is the science of theology, however, not the science of the canonists. For many things pertaining to our faith which are not mentioned in the science of the canonists are found explicitly in theology, but nothing pertaining to the rule of faith can be found in their science except what they receive from theology."

Ockham makes clear that this is not a mere postulate, but something he, and others, affirm:

"...I am aware of some theologians who in their hearts very much look down on canonists of the modern time as being unintelligent, presumptuous, rash, misleading, deceitful, scoffers and ignorant, believing that they do not know the meaning of the sacred canons."

2.

Modern Political Religion

The theological insights of philosophers of First Europe were countered by "political religions." The term "political religion" might strike some as unacceptable. Those who, like those whose lives and ideas we examined in Chapter 1, piously affirmed the tenets of orthodox spiritual traditions and attested to the reality of their faith were countered by intellectual and mass movements. Here we analyze them on the level of engendering "religious experience." There is no lack of scholarship which has identified the religious character of certain political movements.

Norman Cohn's *The Pursuit of the Millennium* (1957), an analysis of medieval European religious movements which is perhaps best known, shows the similarity of these movements to the modern political phenomena of German National Socialism and Communism. These contemporary political ideologies, Cohn shows, are similar in structure to—and in some instances take inspiration from—what we today would call the fanatical, if not irrational, medieval phenomena.

J. L. Talmon's *The Origins of Totalitarian Democracy* (1960) indicates the similarity of the secular apocalyptic strain in 18th-century French philosophy to the chiliastic medieval phenomena. He also traces the revolutionary consequences of this political Messianism in 18th-century France.

Albert Camus' *The Rebel* (1951) analyzes the variants of rebellion in modern speculation and the spiritual character of revolt.

Robert Tucker's *Philosophy and Myth in Karl Marx* (1961) persuasively shows the origins of the thought of Karl Marx in the revolution in religion instituted by Idealist philosophy's creation of an image of man as God.

But perhaps most important for analysis of the nature of modern political religions are the works of Eric Voegelin in which he argues that these political movements are essentially Gnostic. These works principally are *The New Science of Politics* (1952) and *Science, Politics and Gnosticism* (1959).[1]

More recently, Daniel P. Walker and Frances Yates, following the work of Paul Kristeller, have shown the influence of Renaissance Hermeticism in the formation of modern political thought. Utilizing the insights of these studies, especially those dealing with the Gnostic phenomenon,[2] we shall attempt to place in theoretical context the roles of ancient Gnosticism and Renaissance Hermeticism in shaping the modern "Second Realities"[3] of Idealist and atheist humanism.

By "Idealist Humanism," we mean the intellectual movement of philosophic Idealism which dominated European intellectual culture from the publication of Immanuel Kant's *Critique of Pure Reason* (1781) through the first half of the 19th century. By "atheist humanism," we mean the ideological movement created by Ludwig Feuerbach (1804-1872), which culminates in the work of Karl Marx (1818-1883).

Though Idealist and atheist humanism are mutually antagonistic movements, we hope to show by analysis of the "religious" experience which engendered them that they have similar historical roots, equivalent experiential origins, and that they can be analyzed by

---

[1] Originally published as *Wissenschaft, Politik and Gnosis* (Munich: Kosel-Verlag, 1959), English edition, William J. Fitzpatrick, trans. *Science, Politics and Gnosticism. Two Essays.* (Chicago: Henry Refinery Co., Gateway Edition, 1968).

[2] The utility of Gnosticism in analysis of modern thought is examined in Hans Jonas, "Epilogue: Gnosticism, Existentialism, and Nihilism," in *The Gnostic Religion. The Message of the Alien God and the Beginnings of Christianity*, 2nd ed., rev. (Boston: Beacon Press, 1963), 320-340. Other examinations include: John William Corrington, "Charles Reich and the Gnostic Vision," *New Orleans Review*, Vol. 5, No. 1(1976), 3-11; Richard J. Bishirjian, "Carlyle's Political Religion," *Journal of Politics*, Vol. 38 (1976), 95-113; M. E. Bradford, "A Writ of Fire and Sword: The Politics of Oliver Cromwell," *Occasional Review*, Issue 3 (Summer, 1975), 61-80.

[3] Eric Voegelin, "On Debate and Existence," *Intercollegiate Review, III* (1967), 143-152.

reference to their similarity to one another as "Second Realities." The concept "Second Reality" was applied by Eric Voegelin, following Robert Musil, to the attempts to replace reality with another, more acceptable reality originating in the mind of ideologues.

Ancient Gnosticism

Historians dispute the origins of ancient Gnosticism, though it first occurred sometime during the two-hundred-year period from the first century B.C. to the first century A.D. It is not known whether it is pre-Christian, Jewish, or Christian in origin. That in itself is significant because of the condition into which, at that time, the ancient world had fallen. Political disruptions, social upheavals, and military clashes of expanding empires were the normal disruptive conditions for the peoples who, since the expansion of the Persian empire, lived during this period of civilizational unsettlement. As a result of these disorders, traditional religious myths which performed public functions in the maintenance of order of cosmological civilizations lost their social validity and were cast adrift, sometimes to be lost forever or to be adopted in part by conquering cultures.

Sometimes, the old myths were co-opted by the Gnostic sects, plucked from their original symbolic and cultural context and recast into a new form with new meaning. This profusion of symbols has tended to create problems for the scholars in this field, who find it difficult to distinguish among types of Gnosticism.

The word *gnosis is* a Greek word meaning "knowledge." It is different from the word *episteme,* which means science in the sense of human knowledge and the philosophical inquiry into first things. Perhaps with the advent of Gnosticism the word *gnosis* came to mean exclusively religious knowledge, more specifically, secret knowledge of the hidden or alien God.

Hans Jonas writes in *The Gnostic Religion* that the *gnosis* of the Gnostics is truth received through "secret tore or through inner illumination."[4] As such, *gnosis* is knowledge about the god whom man cannot know with his human reason. *Gnosis* was also considered to be an event in the mind of God. Simultaneously with the possession of *gnosis* by the Gnostic, a disruption or existential condition of ignorance in the godhead was resolved. In attempting to define *gnosis,* the Colloquium on the origin of Gnosticism held in Messina in 1966 defined *gnosis* by reference to this ontological function.

Not every *gnosis* is Gnosticism, but only that which involves in this perspective the idea of the divine consubstantiality of the spark that is in need of being awakened and reintegrated. This *gnosis* of Gnosticism involves the divine identity of the *knower* (the Gnostic), the *known* (the divine substance of one's transcendent self), and the *means by which one knows (gnosis* as an implicitly divine faculty is to be awakened and actualized).[5]

The saving character of the possession of gnosis is derived from the belief that the disruption in being which obsessed all Gnostics is not permanent, but is a condition which will pass. They believed that the divine captured in the world and the godhead itself are becoming in a process which will lead to the return of the forces in god to a condition of unity. Gnosticism, therefore, was a prophecy that the contradictions of existence, infinitely radicalized by the Gnostic's rejection of the material world as demonic, would be overcome in a supra-mundane pneumatic process of purification. In a sense, this prophecy of divine unity was self-confirming. The truth of the apocalypse of Gnosticism is known to the Gnostic because he himself is both savior and saved. If the Gnostic's true self were not really divine, he would have remained ignorant; thus the possession of *gnosis* became proof of the revelation. The possession of *gnosis* was also an indication of the superiority of the Gnostic's apocalypse over the revelations of other religions. Mani,

---

[4] Jonas, *The Gnostic Religion,* 35.
[5] Ugo Bianchi, ed., *Le Origini Dello Gnosticismo* (Leiden: E.J. Brill, 1967), xxvii.

for example, the founder of Manichaeanism, claimed to be the fourth and last prophet, the others being Buddha, Zoroaster, and Christ. Gnosticism "transvalued" the values of these earlier theophanies and established with unshakeable certainty the Gnostic's absolute identification of man with God.

We will term this revolutionary attitude, manifest in the identification of *gnosis* with the divine, the syncretism of Gnostic myths, the certainty of their apocalyptic eschatology, and their radical dualism, the "transvaluation of values." The term was coined by Nietzsche, who chose it to express the theme of a projected work, of which only the Preface and the first part, *Der Antichrist*, were completed.[6]

Nietzsche sought to reverse the transvaluation of pagan values which Christianity accomplished by turning the instrument of transvaluation upon Christianity itself. As we use the term, however, we see the instrument as the symbolic form of the type of religious experience characteristic of Gnostic religion. The transvaluation of values signifies, therefore, the reversal and thus implicitly the rejection of traditional valuations of reality. Gnosticism, in this sense, is a radical assertion that what traditional societies have considered true is both untrue and the very essence of evil. This revolutionary significance of Gnostic transvaluation of values is both a major aspect of analysis of Gnosticism and a means of its identification. Gilles Quispel writes in this vein:

> What then is revolutionary in ancient Gnosis? This, that a new outline of the relationship of man to the world and to God is present. The qualitative difference between man and the world is revealed. Man is indeed in the world, however he is not of the world. He is even more than the planet gods which are a cipher, an ideogram of the universe. The world loses its transparency to the divine and becomes daemonic. Plotinus is

---

6 Walter Kaufmann, *The Portable Neitzsche,* 29th ed. (New York: Viking Press, 1970), 568.

amazed to discern that the Gnostics "despised the beauty of the world," something unprecedented for a Greek Man and the world are incommensurable. Man is other than the world and the same as God.[7]

Our discussion of representative Gnostic transvaluations will include their view of matter, cosmos, and man. In the system of Mani, revulsion against matter (a standard theme in Gnosticism, the rejection of physical nature) is explained by means of an elaborate myth in which matter is formed from the carcasses of evil Archons. The plants and the animals which live in the world are the creatures of the evil principle, of Darkness, the result of the lust of evil for light. The system of Valentinus depicts a similar view of matter. The origin of matter is in the emotions of the lowest emanation of the godhead, the Lower Sophia. In one account described by Jonas, the emotions of fear, bewilderment, and ignorance are changed into corporeal form by "Jesus," a saving emanation, sent to the Lowest Sophia by the "Aeons" of the godhead.[8] They are negative and constitute the bad substance, matter. Material existence, for the Gnostics, was not a good, but the epitome of evil.

In ancient philosophy, the concept cosmos symbolizes the experience of order common to man, the order of his soul and of nature *(physis)*; all are expressed in the symbol of the order of the cosmos. Cosmos was also a concept that reflected the totality of order, and the inter-relatedness of order, its commonality, which included in its range the divine, society, nature, and man. Like the symbol of *physis,* which preceded it as the first discovery of philosophy, cosmos is a symbol which included not only the order of the cosmos but the origin of order in the divine.[9] In Gnosticism, the goodness and transparency of cosmic order to the divine is trans-

---

[7] Gilles Quispel, *Gnosis Als Weltreligion* (Zurich: Origo Verlag, 1951), 31.

[8] Jonas, *The Gnostic Religion,* 187-188.

[9] See Eric Voegelin, *The World of the Polis,* 229240, for an interpretation of the fragments of Heraclitus relating to the symbol *cosmos.*

valued. The word ceases to convey the meaning "good order," but now conveys the presence of "evil order." The order of the cosmos to the Gnostics was demonic, the creation of an evil demiurge. The true God, the alien God, is impenetrably beyond the cosmos. Yet it is to Him that the pneumatic essence trapped in the world must return. Hans Jonas writes of the religious attitude fundamental to this view of cosmos:

> We can imagine with what feelings gnostic men must have looked up to the starry sky. How evil its brilliance must have looked to them, how alarming its vastness and the rigid immutability of its courses, how cruel its muteness! The music of the spheres was no longer heard, and the admiration for the perfect spherical form gave place to the terror of so much perfection directed at the enslavement of man. The pious wonderment with which earlier man had looked up to the higher regions of the universe became a feeling of oppression by the iron vault which keeps man exiled from his home beyond. But it is this "beyond" which really qualifies the new conception of the physical universe and of man's position in it. Without it, we should have nothing but a hopeless worldly pessimism. Its transcending presence limits the inclusiveness of the cosmos to the status of only a part of reality, and thus of something from which there is an escape.[10]

What is the psychological center of Gnostic systems? Quispel suggests that it is the condition, existence, and salvation of the trapped spark of the divine.

Gnosis, in the final sense, is anthropology; man stands in the center of the interests of the Gnostics. Their myths and doctrines represent the origin of man and his being, so that he knows which way to go, namely, the way to the self, the way to salvation.[11]

---

[10] Jonas, *The Gnostic Religion*, 261.
[11] Quispel, *Gnosis Als Weltreligion*, 29.

In the strict meaning of the concept "man" as human, not divine, however, they have no interest. What is to be saved is the emanation of the divine trapped in the body. The central theme in Valentinian speculation is the rescue of Adam, the *pneuma* enclosed in matter by the Archons. In the system of Mani, the principle of evil, Darkness, fashions Adam and Eve from the sight of an emanation of the principle of God—into these figures he pours the captive Light of God. The creation of man thus becomes a strategy in the offensive against Good.

We are dealing then with a religion in which the word "man" has two meanings. On the one hand, there is the "man" which is their chief concern and interest. But he is not "man" in the sense that the word implies a theoretical distinction between man and the divine. This "man" is distinctly not human; he is a divine emanation of the godhead. In the Hermetic *Poimandres*, this "man" is Primal Man, an emanation of the "Absolute Power," the image of the "Father."[12] But he aspires to the "power of him who rules over the fire."[13] He is received by the "lower Nature," and this reception explains why "man" is "twofold, mortal through the body, immortal through the essential Man."[14] In nature, "man" is a slave to *heimarmene,* fate, and is ignorant of the Father. Through knowledge "that the Father of all things consists of Light and Life, therefore likewise the Primal Man issued from him, and by this he knows himself to be of Light and Life," and he will return to Life and be saved.[15] There are the knowing ones and the unknowing ones. The unknowing ones are left to be devoured by passions which are evil. Hans Jonas sees in the Hermetic *Poimandres* not just a rejection of the physical universe in the light of pessimism, but the assertion of an entirely new idea of human freedom, very different from the moral conception of it which the Greek philosophers had devel-

---

[12] See Jonas, *The Gnostic Religion,* 148-153, for an examination of Hermetic Gnosticism.

[13] Ibid., 150.

[14] Ibid., 151.

[15] Ibid., 152.

oped. However profoundly man is determined by nature, of which he is part and parcel. . .there still remains an innermost center which is not of nature's realm and by which he is above all its promptings and necessities.[16]

The transvaluation of values of the Gnostics presents substantial problems of theoretical interpretation. Let us compare it to Aristotle's definition of man's humanity. Taking the good man or *spoudaios* as representative man, Aristotle showed the consubstantiality of human *nous* with the divine nous and the actualization of man's humanity in the immortalizing act of noetic contemplation of the divine. This consciousness of the opening of the soul to transcendent *nous* in Greek philosophy is an event in history which offsets or differentiates our creaturely experience of participation in an unchangeable relationship with the divine from the compact experience of being within the medium of the cosmological myths. The new consciousness of transcendence of the divine beyond existence and essence, followed by the discovery of the depth of the human *psyche*, which led in turn to the crucial development of the science of the order of the soul attuned to the divine *arche* of its order, was experienced as an historical development.

This insight into the historical dimension of existence as a process in time was first formulated by Anaximander, who said: "The origin *(arche)* of things is the Apeiron. It is necessary for things to perish into that from which they were born; for they pay one another penalty for their injustice *(adikia)* according to the ordinance of Time."[17] Anaximander experienced existence as a creaturely process which is perishable but nevertheless consubstantial with the timeless Apeiron, which is the origin of the process of existence. Thus Anaximander observes, "it is necessary for things to perish," an acknowledgment, on the one hand, of the reality of death, and, and on the other, of the reality of immortality since what exists will "perish into that from which they were born," which is to say that

---

[16] Ibid., 160.
[17] Quoted in Voegelin, *The Ecumenic Age*, 174.

they will return to the divine *arche* of being. Eric Voegelin writes of this fragment of Anaximander:

> Reality was experienced by Anaximander . . . as a cosmic process in which things emerge from, and disappear into, the nonexistence of the Apeiron. Things do not exist out of themselves, all at once and forever; they exist out of the ground to which they return. Hence, to exist means to participate in two modes of reality: (1) In the Apeiron as the timeless *arche* of things and (2) In the ordered succession of things as the manifestation of the Apeiron in time.[18]

The mystery of reality as a process of participation in the divine origin of being was experienced by the Classical Greek philosophers as a process pointing ultimately towards transfiguration of reality. Plato's concept of the turning around of the *psyche* towards the transcendent Good beyond existence and essence in his *Republic* and St. Augustine's concept of the peregrination of the city of God and the souls of men towards Christ articulate this experience. The ascent *(epanodos)*[19] *of* the soul to the Agathon in Platonic philosophy, just as the conversion of the soul to God of the Christian experience, articulates a transformation of the soul. Yet, this experience did not occlude the simultaneous creaturely experience of the *psyche* in the world. Body which is en-souled is also *psyche* which is embodied. Physical, creaturely existence is reality.

In the Gnostic movement of antiquity in which the scattered diffusion *of* the divine spark ends in a pneumatic process of running back to the godhead, however, this "balance *of* consciousness," to use Eric Voegelin's concept, is lost. The creaturely world is rejected as is the humanity *of* man. Experience of existence as a mode of

---

[18] Ibid. Throughout this section our interpretation has relied on Voegelin's analysis of what he calls the "Balance of Consciousness," *The Ecumenic Age,* Chapter Four, Section 3, 227-238.

[19] Plato, *The Republic,* 529c.

participation is occluded by absolute identification with the divine. The Gnostic experience of the divine, hidden God, from which the Gnostic adept was an emanation, left no room for the noetic experience of the participative nature of human consciousness, of the goodness of the cosmos and of material existence. It left only the transfiguring experience of gnosis.

In 1952, Eric Voegelin, attracted by the similarity of ancient Gnosticism to modern political religions, extended the typology of ancient Gnosticism to an analysis of contemporary political ideologies in order to delimit the religious experience which engendered them. Modern Gnosticism, he found, may be primarily intellectual and assume the form of speculative penetration of the mystery of creation and existence, as, for instance, in the contemplative gnosis of Hegel or Schelling. Or it may be primarily emotional and assume the human soul, as, for instance, in paracletic sectarian leaders. Or it may be primarily volitional and assume the form of activist redemption of man and society, as in the instance of revolutionary activists like Comte, Marx, or Hitler. These Gnostic experiences, in the amplitude of their variety, are the core of the redivinization of society, for the men who fall into these experiences divinize themselves by substituting more massive modes of participation in divinity for faith in the Christian sense.[20]

This modern Gnostic "redivinization of society" is itself a transvaluation of the Christian "dedivinization" of the temporal sphere which was the outcome of the clash between Christianity and pagan culture and its gods. Christian apologists "dedivinized" man and society by expelling the gods from the world. They thus reordered the Western interpretation of man's existence "through the experience of man's destination, by the grace of the world-transcendent God, toward eternal life in beatific vision."[21] This "dedivinization" could not have occurred without the experiential

---

[20] Eric Voegelin, *The New Science of Politics* (Chicago: University of Chicago Press, 1952), 124.

[21] Ibid., 107.

atrophy of polytheism and its challenge in the form of the Christian experience. Thus the contemporary "redivinization" of modern Gnosticism presupposes the atrophy of the Christian experience in intellectual culture and its replacement by a religious experience which is impatient with the uncertainties and anxieties, the insecurity, which accompanies a world without gods.

> . . .when the world is de-divinized, communication with the world-transcendent God is reduced to the tenuous bond of faith, in the sense of Heb. 11:1, as the substance of things hoped for and the proof of things unseen. Ontologically, the substance of things hoped for is. nowhere to be found but in faith itself; and, epistemologically, there is no proof for things unseen but again this very faith. The bond is tenuous, indeed, and it may snap easily. The life of the soul in openness toward God, the waiting, the periods of aridity and dullness, guilt and despondency, contrition and repentance, forsakenness and hope against hope, the silent stirrings of love and grace, trembling on the verge of a certainty *which* if gained is loss-the very lightness of this fabric may prove too heavy a burden for men who lust for massively possessive experience.[22]

Voegelin's experiential analysis of the Gnostic character of political ideologies was based on several generations of scholarship, commencing with the nineteenth century student of Gnosticism, Ferdinand Christian Baur, Professor of Theology at the University of Tübingen, who devoted Part Four of his work *Die Christliche Gnosis, oder die Religionsphilosophie in ihrergeschichtlichen Entwicklung*[23] to a comparison of ancient Gnosticism with the theosophy of Boehme, Schelling's philosophy of nature, Schleiermacher's doctrine of faith, and Hegel's philosophy of religion.

Since 1952, however, more recent research has persuaded

---

[22] Ibid., 122.
[23] Tubingen, 1835.

Voegelin that analysis of modern political religion under the generic term "gnosticism" tends to obscure the historical complexity of this phenomenon. Other streams of religious thought, particularly including Hermeticism, "demonic magic" and NeoPlatonism, Kabbalah, and Alchemy, were impotent contributors to the development of modern intellectual consciousness.[24]

Our purpose in what remains of this chapter will be to show how two aspects of the Gnostic derailment, occlusion of creaturely existence and absolute identification of "man" with God, became formative elements in the shaping of modern political religion. For this reason, we will examine the phenomenon of Renaissance Hermeticism by which, in part, the Gnostic deification of man was transmitted to the modern world. We will attempt to differentiate the Gnostic elements in Hermeticism from the non-Gnostic and then try to show how these two movements were important contributory elements in the development of philosophic Idealism.

Renaissance Humanism

The revival of the thought of Hermes Trismegistus by the Renaissance Neo-Platonists was not as strange a renascence as one might think. The Renaissance itself is noted for its high valuation of the past, and the thought of Hermes Trismegistus was believed to constitute an ancient revelation predating the revelation of Moses and the philosophy of the Greeks. By reviving the *prisca theologia* (antique theology) of Hermes, early Renaissance Neo-Platonists like Marsilio Ficino (1433-1499) attempted to revive a true ancient theology and reconcile it with Christianity. That later persons like

---

[24] See Eric Voegelin, "On Hegel-A Study in Sorcery," *Studium Generale,* 24 (1971), 335-368; "On Debate and Existence, "*Intercollegiate Review,* II (1967) 143-152; idem, "The Eclipse of Reality," in Maurice Natanson, ed., *Phenomenology and Social Reality: Essays in Memory* of *Alfred Schutz* (The Hague, Martinus Nijhoff, 1970), 185-194. Also in this line of redefinition is Part Two of Thomas Molnar, *God and the Knowledge of Reality* (New York: Basic Books, Publishers, 1973), 73-143.

Giordano Bruno would abandon this Christian interpretation and simply assert the truth of Hermeticism was the natural outgrowth of a radical antiphilosophical testament. When in 1614 Isaac Casaubon demonstrated by textual analysis that the Hermetic writings were in fact post-Christian in origin, fanatic devotees of Hermeticism rejected the evidence. Committed to the reform of religion by an infusion of the thought of Hermes, the new Renaissance messiahs were not deflected from their redemptive paths by a scholarly argument that the documents on which their new religion was based were not what they believed them to be. The central focus of the Gnostic aspects of ancient Hermeticism was the deification of man. In the *Poimandres* of Hermes Trismegistus, an account of a mystic vision in which the mind of God, identified as Poimandres, speaks directly to Hermes, the transmission of divine gnosis is made possible because that which Hermes is able to see and hear of the divine *nous is* itself divine.[25] Those who attain to this knowledge are saved by becoming God.

In Hermetic thought, man has two souls: "the one is from the First Mind and also shares in the power of the Demiurge, the other has been put in from the revolution of the heavens, and into this the God-seeing soul enters."[26] Thus, the lower soul embodies the higher or "God-seeing soul," and the function of gnosis is to release the higher from the lower. Ontologically, that which is saved by gnosis is the god which saves. Embodied in this deification of man is a radically new idea of the freedom of man. If in the philosophic sense freedom is action within certain moral limits, the essence of freedom in the Hermetic sense is the overcoming of limits.

The core of Renaissance Hermeticism as in ancient Gnosticism was a radical deification of man, with similar anthropological consequences. The ideas which Marsilio Ficino used to express this were several. In its most general form, he used the concept of the circle: the beginning and end of which is God, the middle, human

---

[25] Jonas, *The Gnostic Religion*, 149.
[26] Ibid., 160.

intellect.[27] Alternatively, he wrote of the existence of the "divine mind" in men, living, shining, and reflecting itself there".[28] This concept of the dwelling of the divine mind in man may simply be a way of expressing the idea that all that is exists in God. But Ficino wrote further that man is the image of God in the sense that his true being is a reflection of the "divine face" or divine goodness. God, he wrote, in willing himself, "wills all other things which are God Himself as being in God, and as flowing out of God are images of the divine face and have as their end the task of reproducing and confirming the divine goodness."[29]

The symbol of the "flowing out" or emanation of existent things in God tends to break the distinction of kind between creaturely existence and the divine and alter it to a difference of degree. Consequently, Ficino could write that if God is goodness, then the soul becomes God by love of goodness.[30] "Just as, not he who sees the good, but he who wills it becomes good, so the Soul becomes divine. not from considering God, but from loving Him."[31] Ficino writes also, "The entire effort of our Soul is to become God. This effort is as natural to man as that of flying is to birds. For it is inherent in all men, everywhere and always; therefore it does not follow the incidental quality of some man, but the nature of the species itself."[32]

Giovanni Pico della Mirandola also expressed these ideas, though more compactly and allegorically, in his "Oration on the Dignity of Man." Written as a preface or introductory speech to the publication of his nine hundred theses, this short oration is a virtual

---

[27] Paul Oskar Kristeller, *The Philosophy of Marsilio Ficino,* Virginia Conant, trans. (reprint of 1943 ed.; Gloucester, Mass.: Peter Smith, 1964), 100.

[28] Ibid., 79.

[29] Ibid., 145.

[30] Ibid., 264.

[31] Ibid., 269.

[32] Ibid., 337.

compendium of the Hermetic deification of man.[33] Unfortunately, the disputation which was to occur in Rome in January 1487 never took place because an alert Pope Innocent VIII, suspecting the heretical cast of some of Giovanni Pico's theses, prohibited the disputation and ordered an investigation.

The somewhat restricted Christian Hermeticism of Ficino and Giovanni Pico gave place in the late sixteenth century to the aggressive revival of Hermetic *prisca theologia* by Giordano Bruno. Bruno was accused of saying that he intended to "found a new sect under the name of philosophy," a form of competition frowned upon by the Inquisitors who burned him at the stake in 1600. Bruno viewed himself as a Messiah come to save the world through a renaissance of Hermetic magic. In his *Spaccio della bestia trionfante* (1584), Bruno openly advocates the making of "familiar, affable and domestic gods,"[34] as the means of world renewal. In that work, Jupiter admonishes the other gods to reform themselves, promising that "if we thus renew our heaven, the constellations and influences shall be new, the impressions and fortunes shall be new, for all things depend on this upper world."[35]

The magician participates in this celestial renewal by divinations which evoke the good traits of the gods and thus simultaneously reduce the influence of their bad traits.[36] This attitude conflicts with the ancient Gnostic antipathy to the material world, but the Hermetic corpus also contained the basically non-Gnostic religious view of the world as a manifestation of God.

It was this acceptance of the world in a transfigured state, but

---

[33] A translation of Giovanni Pico's "Oration" is available in E. Cassirer, P.O. Kristeller, J.H. Randall, Jr., eds. *The Renaissance Philosophy of Man* (Chicago: University of Chicago Press, 1948), 223-254.

[34] Frances Yates, *Giordano Bruno and the Hermetic Tradition* (Chicago: University of Chicago Press, 1964), 212. For an examination of "demonic magic in Renaissance Hermetism," see *also D.P. Walker, Spiritual and Demonic Magic from Ficino to Campanella* (London: Warburg Institute, University of London, 1958).

[35] Yates, *Giordano Bruno*, 218.

[36] Ibid., 221-222.

not in its present reality, which, we believe, was a principal formative element in the view of nature of Idealist Humanism. In one
aspect of the *Corpus Hermeticum,* for example, the world is viewed as
transparent to a world spirit or God which itself images forth the
"greater god."[37]   All beings in the world are by that token in God.
In the "Lament" of the Hermetic *Asclepius,* the view of imminent
decline is coupled with the view of world reform. In the old age of
the world, evil, as opposed to good, will prevail, the gods will de-
part from man, and the order of nature will collapse. But this condition is not final. At some point in this decline, God will intervene
by means of a flood or consuming fire that will destroy evil, and the
world will be returned to its original beauty. "That is what the re-
birth of the world will be; a renewal of all good things, a holy and
most solemn restoration of Nature herself, imposed by force in the
course of time...by the will of God."[38] Perhaps persuaded that culture was undergoing a process of renewal, the Renaissance Magus
found this Hermetic view quite appealing since he viewed his own
action to be somehow participating in a greater process of world
renewal. Underlying Renaissance Hermeticism is a subtle change
from the Medieval understanding of man, the seeds of which were
sown in Hellenistic Hermeticism.

What has changed is Man, now no longer only the pious spectator of God's wonders in the creation, and worshipper of God
himself above the creation, but Man the operator, Man who seeks
to draw power from the divine and natural order.[39]

Frances Yates and Paul Kristeller see the immediate influence
of the Hermeticism of Ficino and Bruno in "Galileo's claim that
man's knowledge of mathematics is different in quantity but not in
kind from that of God Himself;" in the natural magic of Shakespeare's plays; the political theory and action of Campanella; the
growth of Rosicrucianism and perhaps Freemasonry; Sir Thomas

---

[37] Ibid., 33.
[38] Ibid., 39-40.
[39] Ibid., 144.

Moore's critique of Cartesian naturalism; and Francis Bacon's *New Atlantis.*[40] The influence of Hermetic gnosticism did not terminate in the early seventeenth century, however. We hope to show certain similarities between Renaissance Hermeticism and philosophical Idealism.

Idealist Humanism

The origin of Idealist Humanism as an identifiable ideological movement may be found, Robert Tucker indicates, in Immanuel Kant's (1724-1804) "expression of a compulsion in man to achieve absolute moral self-perfection."[41] As we have seen, however, there are traces of such a deification of man in Rousseau's "legislator," and even earlier in Machiavelli's prince. Thus, we believe that Tucker's placement of the origins of Idealist Humanism in Immanuel Kant is much too late. The origins of Idealist Humanism, we believe, lie in the Renaissance revival of the Gnosticism and pantheism of Hermes Trismegistus. Nevertheless, Tucker is correct in seeing Kant as an advocate of a view of man as godlike. Adopting Kant's distinctions between "noumenon," a thing not an object of sense experience, and "phenomena," objects of sense experience as they appear in consciousness, Tucker attributes to Kant a view of man as a "divided being a dual personality: *homo noumenon* and *homo phenomenon.*"[42] *Homonoumenon* is man's real self, of which *homo phenomenon* is only an appearance. Man is thus torn between what he really is and what he appears to be, but really is not completely. Kant, Tucker writes, portrays man in a posture of anguished striving to actualize an image of himself as divinely virtuous. He writes that there would be no need for morality at all, no obligation or

---

[40] Paul Oskar Kristeller, *Renaissance Concepts of 'Man and Other Essays'* (New York: Harper Torchbooks, Harper and Row, Publishers, 1972), 20; *Yates, Giordano Bruno*, 357; 360-397; 413; 274; 427; 450.

[41] Robert Tucker, *Philosophy and Myth in Karl Marx* (Cambridge: At The University Press 1965), 33.

[42] Ibid., 34.

"moral compulsion," if man were in actual fact a "holy being." This is a manner of suggesting that morality is the compulsion to become such a holy being in actual act. It is a compulsion to become godlike.[43]

Other passages in Kant's works support such an interpretation. In the *Critique of Practical Reason,* for example, Kant writes that moral law leads us to religion because religion recognizes duties as divine commands. Our own moral action, then, must be conceived as an attempt to harmonize our own will with that of God's, even though such harmony cannot be attained by finite beings.[44] Kant writes in the *Groundwork of the Metaphysics of Morals* that our ideal will which makes universal laws is the proper object of reverence.[45] Kant also saw man's will as his "proper" or real self, and this he called the "divine man within us."[46]

One of the political consequences of an anthropology such as Kant's is to make "autonomy"[47] the essential end of politics.

A good man is an autonomous man, and for him to realize his autonomy, he must be free. Self-determination thus becomes the supreme political good. For its sake Kant is prepared to accept brutality; to it he subordinates all the other benefits of social life; self-government, as a well-known slogan was later to put it, is better

---

[43] Ibid., 33.

[44] Ibid.

[45] Immanuel Kant, *Groundwork of the Metaphysic of Morals,* H.J. Paton, trans. (New York: Harper and Row, Publishers, Harper Torchbooks, The Academy Library, 1964), 105.

[46] *Ibid., 126; idem, Immanuel Kant's Critique of Pure Reason,* Norman Kemp Smith, trans. (New York: St. Martin's Press, 1965), 486. In Kant's posthumously published notes he wrote, "God must be represented not as a substance outside me, but as the highest moral principle in me. The idea of that which human reason itself makes out of the World. All is the active representation of God. Not as a special personality, substance outside me, but as a thought in me." Quoted in Thomas Molnar, God and the Knowledge of Reality (New York: Basic Books, Inc. Publishers, 1973), 166.

[47] Elie Kedourie, *Nationalism,* 3rd ed. (London: Hutchinson University Library, 1974), 29.

than a good government.[48]

A basic timorousness or scepticism in his work, however, limited what otherwise would have been a tendency towards dogmatic political action in Kant himself. His dictum that the "thing-in-itself" cannot be known had first to be overcome if a radical political doctrine was to be formulated on Kantian territory. This breakthrough was, of course, not long in coming. Though Kant would argue that of "things-in-themselves," we can know only their appearances, the limitations thus imposed on critical philosophy were too restrictive to satisfy the intellectual appetites of Georg Wilhelm Hegel (1770-1831). The Kantian categories of pure reason, Hegel argued, are unfit for speculative thought, which must of necessity ascend to the Absolute.[49] Of Kant's admonition against attempting to know things-in-themselves, Hegel writes, "On the contrary, there is nothing we can know so easily."[50] "Absolute idealism," he thought, went far beyond the "subjective idealism" of Kant because it allows us to know the identity of the Absolute, to know the. "thing-in-itself," to know the nature of God.[51] This assertion creates problems. For if ultimately the object of science is to know God as He knows himself, then the one who knows is required to become like God. For the enterprise to succeed, the distinction between man and God must be cast aside and replaced with a man-god.

The Idealist View of Man as God

Like the Renaissance Hermeticists and ancient Gnostics, Hegel was persuaded that man was essentially divine and consequently

---

[48] Ibid., 29-30.

[49] G. W. Hegel, *The Logic of Hegel Translated from the Encyclopaedia of the Philosophical Sciences,* William Wallace, trans., 2nd ed. rev. (London: Oxford University Press, 1972), 91 (hereafter cited as Hegel, *Encyclopaedia*).

[50] Ibid., 92.

[51] Ibid., 93; idem, *Hegel's Lectures on the History of Philosophy,* E.S. Haldane, trans., 3 vols. (New York: Humanities Press, Inc., 1955), I:71.

was troubled by the effect upon what he viewed as the Christian religion "if human nature is absolutely severed from the divine, if no mediation between the two is conceded except in one isolated individual, if all man's consciousness of the good and the divine is degraded to the dull and killing belief in a superior Being altogether alien to man."[52] Apparently, the divinity of Christ, if that excluded the divinity of all men and gave to Christ alone the role of mediator between God and man, was too much for the young Hegel, who could not accept that man and God were different in kind. On this same subject he wrote:

> The hill and the eye which sees it are object and subject, but between man and God, between spirit and spirit, there is no such cleft of objectivity and subjectivity; one is to the other an other only in that one recognizes the other; both are one.[53]

What motivates such a formulation? It was in his *Lectures on the History of Philosophy* that Hegel said his only desire was to know the nature of God.[54] Yet, if man himself is divine, is that not an aspiration to know oneself? Hegel's discussion of the story of Adam in the *Encyclopaedia* in which he touches upon the role philosophy must play in a world composed of essentially divine men is suggestive of such an aspiration:

> We are further told, God said, "Behold Adam is become as one of us, to know good and evil." Knowledge is now spoken of as divine *(das Gottliche)* and not, as before, as something wrong and forbidden. Such words contain a confutation of the *idle talk that philosophy pertains only to the finitude of the mind.* Philos-

[52] G. W. Hegel, *On Christianity: Early Theological Writings,* T.M. Knox, trans. (New York: Harper and Brothers, Harper Torchbooks, Cloister Library, 1961), 176.
[53] Ibid., 265.
[54] Hegel, *Lectures on the History of Philosophy, I:71.*

ophy is knowledge, and *it is through knowledge that man first realizes his original vocation, to be the image of God (ein Ebenbild Gottes zu sein).*[55]

Hegel is clearly saying that philosophy is not the means by which we manifest our love of truth. It is the vehicle of our *libido* to become "the image of God." Man, of course, is not *"the* image of God," in the sense in which Hegel intends it as the *exact* image (*Ebenbild),* unless Hegel was referring to an account, other than that in Genesis which speaks of the Elohim having decided to make man *"in* our image." The crucial difference between Genesis 1:26 and Hegel's formulation is the difference between the Hermetic-Gnostic view, which identifies man with God absolutely (that is, sees him as divine), and the Classical-Christian view, which sees him as a spiritual but imperfect *human* being.

Hegel's interpretation of the account of Christ's transfiguration is also of interest because its focus is not on Christ or the amazement of his witnesses, but rather on its ramifications for Peter's vocation as a type of clairvoyance.

After Peter had recognized Jesus as divine in nature and thereby proved that he had a sense of the whole depth of man because he had been able to take a man as a son of God, Jesus gave over to him the power of the keys of the Kingdom of Heaven. What he bound was to be bound in Heaven, and what he loosed was to be loosed in Heaven, also. Since Peter had become conscious of a God in *one* man, he must also have been able to recognize in anyone else the divinity or non-divinity of his being, or to recognize it in a third party (*in einem Dritten*) as that party's sensing of divinity or non divinity, *i.e.,* as the strength of that party's belief or disbelief.[56]

Peter's clairvoyance pertains to his ability to see God in other men who had faith. But faith in what? The passage suggests that Peter's faith was in himself and, to the degree that he too was di-

---

[55] Hegel, *Encyclopaedia,* 56. Emphasis added.
[56] Hegel, *On Christianity: Early Theological Writings,* 242.

vine, in himself as God.

Hegel shared this view of man with Johann Fichte (1762-1814), who, especially in his later popular works, extended his inquiry beyond the critical development of problems in Idealism to exhortative expositions of the "self" as identical with the divine and thus made the "self" the foundation of Idealist speculation. Yet even in his earlier work, the *Wissenschaftslehre* (1794), it is clear that Fichte's concept of the "self," the "*Ich*," is not restricted to the conscious intellect.

Fichte saw a fundamental duality in the self, between the self which posits itself and the self which is posited. His identification of self-positing with reflection, which he called the act of the infinite self, restricted the understanding of Idealist Humanists of philosophical consciousness to consciousness of an infinite self which is the creator of the finite self. Fichte collapsed the distinction in reality between existence and being, immanence and transcendence, by including within one concept, the self, all reality. "The self demands that it encompass all reality and exhaust the infinite. This demand of necessity rests on the idea of the absolutely posited, *infinite* self; and this is the *absolute* self, of which we have been talking.[57]

Fichte's concept of a self which has burst the limitations of human consciousness and become infinite led Emile Brehier in his essay on Fichte in *The Nineteenth Century: Period of Systems, 1800-1850* to suggest that Fichte's concept of the self can be understood as "a kind of metaphysical Manicheism."[58] By this Brehier meant that the pre-existent opposition between light and darkness, good and evil, which is the chief characteristic of Manichaean systems, is conceptually equivalent to Fichte's exposition of the interplay between infinite and finite self. As in the system of Mani, he argued, the focus of Fichte's thought lies in the ultimate triumphal resolution of hos-

---

[57] Johann Gottlieb Fichte, *Science of Knowledge,* Peter Heath and John Lachs, trans. (New York: Appleton-Century-Crofts, 1970), 244.

[58] Emile Brehier, *The Nineteenth Century: Period of Systems, 1800-1850,* Wade Baskin, trans. (Chicago: University of Chicago press, 1968), 122.

tile forces in the absolute ego.

These sentiments with their peculiar Gnostic cast ultimately cropped up in the work of the early English interpreter of German Idealism, Thomas Carlyle (1795-1881), who wrote in one of his essays:

> "Neither say thou that proper Realities are wanting: for Man's Life, now, as of old, is the genuine work of God; wherever there is a Man, a God also is revealed, and all that is Godlike: a whole epitome of the Infinite, with its meanings, lies enfolded in the Life of every Man. Only, alas, that the Seer to discern this same Godlike, and with fit utterance unfold it for us, is wanting, and may long be wanting."[59]

This passage, like that of Hegel, intentionally mixes the Genesis account of man as made ("'the genuine work of God'") in the image of God, with the Hermetic-Gnostic idea that man is literally God ("'wherever there is a Man, a God also is revealed'"). In *Heroes and Hero-Worship,* Carlyle recalled Novalis' assertion, "'There is but one Temple in the Universe. . .and that is the Body of Man.'"[60] This quotation is paralleled in the same passage by a fragment attributed to St. John Chrysostom, "The True Shekinah is Man!" In non-Kabbalistic Jewish tradition the *Shekhinah* means God himself. Interpreting the above sentence in this sense, we read, "The true God is Man," a statement clearly unacceptable to orthodox Judaism, but consistent with the Gnosticism of the Kabbalah.[61]

---

[59] Thomas Carlyle, *The Works of Thomas Carlyle in Thirty Volumes,* H.D. Traill, ed., Centenary Edition (London: Chapman and Hall, Ltd., 1896-1899), XXVIII, 52. For an assessment of the gnosticism of English Idealism, see Richard J. Bishirjian, "Thomas Hill Green's Political Philosophy," *Political Science Reviewer,* Vol. IV (Fall, 1974), 29-53. Also see *idem,* "Carlyle's Political Religion," Vol. 38, *Journal of Politics, V, 10.*

[60] Carlyle, *Works,* V, 10.

[61] Our understanding of the Gnosticism of the Kabbalah is derived from Gershom G. Scholem, *On The Kabbalah and Its Symbolism* (New York:

Atheist Humanism

Just as the ancient Gnostics, Renaissance Hermeticists, and Idealist Humanists rejected man's humanity in the assertion of his divinity, atheist humanism destroyed God in order to emphasize the "true" power of man. The former movements asserted man's radical divinity, the latter that man himself was God, which, in terms diametrically opposed, is the same "truth." Atheist humanism is the mirror-like opposite reflection of Idealist Humanism.

This relationship is due in part, perhaps, to the nature of philosophical revolutions which tend to assert a position at the opposite extreme from the presently dominant school. But it may also be due, we suggest, to the presence of an equivalent engendering experience.

Ancient Gnosticism sought escape from a condition of unacceptable existence by the return of the divine spark to a radically hidden god. From the Gnostic perspective of a demonic world, both the world and man are rejected in the total absorption of consciousness in a hidden divine reality. The equilibrium of Classical Greek philosophy in which man came to know his creaturely place in being by noetic experience of his participation in the divine *nous* is replaced with the Gnostic's consuming experience of identification with a radically transcendent god.

Alternatively, the modern movements of Renaissance Hermeticism, Idealist Humanism, and atheist humanism project the unity of divine completeness *into* this world in a vision of a world free of contradictions. Both worlds of the Gnostics and of the modern political religions are, of course, "Second Realities," for man and the world are not demonic, but are consubstantial with the divine. Nor is the world wholly divine or capable of becoming divine in some process of world immanent renovation. These modern movements, however, represent a revolt against reality which they con-

Schocken Books, 1969), 104-105.

strue as defective, with the distinction that in atheist humanism this revolt has reached its fullest historical development, not in the spiritual terms of the preceding movements, but in a radically desacralized mode. Atheist humanism is the secularization of the vision of Renaissance Hermeticism and philosophical Idealism of a totally spiritualized world. What is imminent in history, the Atheist humanist believes, is a brave new exclusively material, though reconstituted, existence.

Fr. Henri DeLubac, S.J., coined the term "atheist humanism"[62] to classify the disparate thought of those intellectuals who represented the new development of a type of humanism based on the view that man is an autonomous being, independent of any obligation to a higher order because man is self-creating, that is, his own creator. Like Albert Camus, who observed that "to become God is to accept crime,"[63] Fr. Lubac criticized atheist humanism for having led to the actual annihilation of human beings. An intellectual movement which began by displacing God led not to the actualization of man's humanity, but to the release of men from the limits which would have restrained them from murdering their fellow human beings in the name of humanity. Below the atheist humanist's reduction of all reality to the material and the rejection of the spiritual aspects of man's humanity lay an engendering impulse to possess totally or master reality perceived as alien. This *libido dominandi,* this lust for power, Fr. Lubac argued, was essentially religious. Though atheist humanists were anti-religious, they were so in a furiously religious way which tended to obscure a deeper moral or spiritual choice to live in a cosmos in which the only god is man. In Idealist Humanism, man is believed to be actually divine; in the world of atheist humanism, absent of divine reality, man becomes god by default.

---

[62] Henri De Lubac, *The Drama of Atheist Humanism,* Edith M. Riley, trans. (Cleveland: World Publishing Co., Meridian Books, 1965).

[63] Albert Camus, *The Rebel,* Anthony Bower, trans. (New York: Random House, Vintage Books, 1961), 59.

Ludwig Feuerbach: Idealist Humanism began as a movement with Renaissance Hermeticism and Passed through Kant, Schiller, Fichte, Schelling, and Hegel. With Hegel's death in 1831, it ceased to develop further in the reflective channels in which it formerly flowed. The peculiar mixture of philosophy and theology in Idealist Humanism which constituted a revolution in religion led to a religion of revolution. The man whose works marks this transition in modern political religions was Ludwig Feuerbach (1804-1872), a student of Hegel.

Feuerbach felt that the moment in which he lived was a new epoch, the "epoch of the downfall of Christianity."[64] The place of belief has been taken by unbelief and that of the Bible by reason. Similarly, religion and the Church have been replaced by politics, the heaven by the earth, prayer by work, hell by material need, and the Christian by man.[65] Given this fact of Western culture, Feuerbach advocated that the epoch of the downfall of Christianity be brought to its completion by placing man in the position formerly occupied by God. Only thus can we free ourselves from the contradiction that is at present poisoning our innermost being—the contradiction between our life and thought on one hand, and a religion that is fundamentally opposed to them on the other. *For religious we must once again become if politics is to become our religion.*[66]

The new god of the religion of politics, of an orientation utterly this-worldly, could only be man. Throughout Feuerbach's works, this atheist insight is stated, restated, expounded, elaborated upon, and further developed. Perhaps because this was the *idee fixe* of his intellection, if not his psychological obsession, no scholar has argued that Feuerbach stands in the first rank of nineteenth century philosophy.

---

[64] Ludwig Feuerbach, "The Necessity of a Reform Philosophy," *The Fiery Brook: Selected Writings of Ludwig Feuerbach,* Zawar Hanfi, trans . (Garden City, New York: Anchor Books, Doubleday and Co., Inc., 1972), 147.

[65] Ibid., *148*-149.

[66] Ibid., 149. Emphasis added.

Karl Barth, in his "introductory Essay" to a new edition of Feuerbach's *The Essence of Christianity*, calls this principal thesis "almost nauseatingly, trivial."[67] All the same, Feuerbach's impact on the group of radical Hegelians, which included Karl Marx, was striking. This influence was due to both the new atheist humanism of Feuerbach and to its corollary, his critique of philosophical Idealism.

In "Towards a Critique of Hegel's Philosophy," Feuerbach argued that Hegel had imprisoned the intellect in a system of reason,[68] which was not immediate intellection, the "intellect within us," but abstract reason, a lifeless fabrication of reason in its concrete form. Similarly, in his "Preliminary Theses on the Reform of Philosophy," Feuerbach argued that Hegelian philosophy had "alienated man *from himself*" by positing "the *essence* of man outside of man."[69] Karl Marx, following Feuerbach, wrote:

> Free yourselves from the concepts and prepossession of existing speculative philosophy if you want to get at things differently, as they are, that is to say, if you want to arrive at the truth. And there is no other road for you to truth and freedom except that leading through the stream of fire. Feuerbach is the purgatory of the present times.[70]

What are the characteristics of Feuerbach's atheist humanism? Feuerbach thought that every being is infinite.[71] In "Towards a Critique of Hegel's Philosophy," he wrote, "The being of man is no longer a particular and subjective, but a universal being, for man has

---

[67] Ludwig Feuerbach, *The Essence of Christianity*, George Eliot, trans. (New York: Harper and Row, Publishers, Harper Torchbooks, The Cloister Library, 1957), xix.

[68] Feuerbach, *The Fiery Brook*, 68.

[69] Ibid., 157.

[70] Quoted in David McLellan, *Marx Before Marxism* (New York: Harper Torchbooks, Harper and Row, Publishers, 1971), 108.

[71] Feuerbach, *The Essence of Christianity*, 38.

the whole universe as the object of his drive for knowledge."[72] Man lusts to know, he actualizes himself in his drive to know the universe, and this actuality for Feuerbach is the sign that man is not limited. "Reason is existence objective to itself as its own end; the ultimate tendency of things. That which is an object to itself is the highest, the final being; that, which has the power over itself is almighty."[73]

In criticism, Karl Barth wrote that Feuerbach ignored two important realities in this assertion: man will die, and man is evil. That Feuerbach ignored such basic realities "accounts for the shallowness of his explanation of religion."[74] Nevertheless, this drive for knowledge was the foundation of Feuerbach's political thought. Christianity, by displacing man's true humanity in a transcendent God, gave Christians another-worldly orientation. Their "republic" was in heaven; thus, they did not need one here in this world. With the abolition of Christianity, man could now find paradise in this world. That shift would require a philosophy which had transvalued the *summum bonum* of Christian philosophy.

In the new epoch which is to replace the Christian, we will have "the right to constitute a republican state."[75] For speculative thought, *man,* Feuerbach wrote, is the *summum bonum.* This anthropological view he called "anthropotheism,"[76] a philosophy which sees man as the ground of being. In the age given to atheist humanism, therefore, the state will perform the role in the development of mankind as an "infinite being."[77] The role was equivalent to providence, he thought, creating a context of universality for men who see themselves as the ultimate reality. It is therefore this practical

---

[72] Feuerbach, "Towards a Critique of Hegel's Philosophy," *The Fiery Brook,* 93.

[73] Feuerbach, *The Essence of Christianity,* 43.

[74] Ibid., xxviii.

[75] Feuerbach, "The Necessity of a Reform of Philosophy," *The Fiery Brook,* 152.

[76] "Preliminary Theses on the Reform of Philosophy," Ibid., 166.

[77] "The Necessity of a Reform of Philosophy," Ibid., 150.

atheism that provides the states with what holds them together; human beings come together in the state because here they are without God, because the state is their god, which is why it can justifiably claim for itself the divine predicate of "majesty."[78]

With acute psychological insight, Feuerbach saw that politics would become a type of religion for men who rejected Christianity because it stifled their lust to actualize their "true" nature in political action.

Karl Marx (1818-1883): The new religion of atheist humanism was adopted by Karl Marx, who followed Feuerbach in his rejection of Christianity. Yet Marx would go further than Feuerbach, whom he criticized for his "idealism,"[79] because he had not completely shaken himself free from Hegel's yoke. Feuerbach spoke of man, but did not realize, Marx said, that man is a "social product."[80] There was much good in Feuerbach, of course, but Marx was critical because, he said,. Feuerbach never went beyond "isolated surmises."[81] Nevertheless, Marx concurred in Feuerbach's criticism of theology.

In notes to his doctoral dissertation Marx argued that ontological proofs of the existence of God are merely proofs of the existence of *"human self-consciousness."*[82] In his "Economic and Philosophic Manuscripts," he wrote that gods are only the effect of "an aberration of the human mind."[83] Yet, he was perplexed by the theological question of origins first asked by the Greek natural philosophers to the extent that he refused to grapple with the philosophical problems it proposed. We must expel the notion of creation of

---

[78] Ibid.

[79] For the sake of economy, we restrict our references here to the period of the "Young Marx," which covers the years from 1838-1846. Karl Marx, *The German Ideology,* in *Writings of the Young Marx on Philosophy and Society,* Loyd D. Easton and Kurt H. Guddat, trans. and eds. (Garden City, New York: Anchor Books, Doubleday & Company, Inc., 1967), 419.

[80] "Theses on Feuerbach," Ibid., 402.

[81] The German Ideology, Ibid., 416.

[82] Ibid., 65.

[83] Ibid., 298.

the world, he said, for Man is his own self creator. If we do not, then we must logically admit that man is not autonomous.

Marx was spiritually unprepared to accept what he could not honestly deny: that man could not have created himself. So, he called the philosophical question of the *arche* of being an "abstraction."[84] Abstractions, such as the question of genesis, says Marx, have become impossible for "socialist man." Socialist man "has evident and incontrovertible proof of his self *creation,* his own *formation process.*"[85] The willful assertion of a new type of man who turns his back on philosophy in the knowledge that he creates himself is the basis of Marx's humanism and his "communism."

Marx wanted to go beyond the critique of religion to engage in actual revolution. In the "Theses on Feuerbach," he wrote, "The philosophers have *only interpreted* the world in various ways; the point is, to *change* it."[86] Like many of his generation for whom a scholarly career was not the traditional means by which to master an intellectual discipline and impart it to the next generation, Marx instead wanted to change the world by radically revolutionary means. The basis of his concept of revolution was his anthropology.

"Man," he wrote, *"lives* by nature," in the sense that nature was an autonomous realm, independent of any higher order. Thus, to live by nature "means that nature is his *body* with which he must remain in perpetual process in order not to die. That the physical and spiritual life of man is tied up with nature is another way of saying that nature is linked to itself, for man is a part of nature."[87] As a "species-being" man's labor is an end in itself, by which Marx meant that man's relationship to nature produces man as an "active species-life."[88] The object of labor is thus the *objectification of man's*

---

84 Ibid., 313.
85 Ibid., 314.
86 Ibid., 402.
87 "Economic and Philosophic Manuscripts," Ibid., 293.
88 Ibid., 295.

species-life: he produces himself not only intellectually, as in consciousness, but also actively in a real sense and sees himself in a world he made."[89] Because in bourgeois society man is alienated from his labor by capital and private property, man lives in a condition of alienation. This analysis of estrangement formed the basis of Marx's call for a revolution which would liberate man as a species from the destruction he experiences in presently constituted society.

Marx develops his theory of revolution in *The German Ideology* (1845-46). Because "communism" is the restoration of man, he writes, "Communism is for us not a *state of affairs* still to be established, not an *ideal* to which reality (will) have to adjust. We call communism the *real* movement which abolishes the present state of affairs."[90] By abolishing private property, "the liberation of each single individual will be accomplished to *the* extent that history becomes world history."[91] The class that will carry out this liberation is the class, which, in the pronounced degradation of man by the development of the productive forces that subjugate it, develops "communist consciousness." Such a practical revolutionary consciousness, not criticism, is "the driving force of history.[92]

This communism as completed naturalism is humanism, as completed humanism it is naturalism. It is the *genuine* resolution of the antagonism between man and nature and between man and man; it is the true resolution of the conflict between existence and essence, objectification and self-affirmation, freedom and necessity, individual and species. It is the riddle of history solved and knows itself as this solution.[93]

Marx has created a political religion based on the metastatic expectation that a violent revolution will overcome the contradictions of human existence. As such, there are difficulties with his formula. Marx claimed his "communism" was "scientific." In the "Econom-

---

[89] Ibid.
[90] Ibid., 426.
[91] Ibid., 429.
[92] Ibid., 432.
[93] "Economic and Philosophic Manuscripts," Ibid., 304.

ic and Philosophical Manuscripts," he based his conclusions on what he believed were economic analyses of political economy; but, as we have suggested, they are actually the conclusions appropriate to a radical atheist anthropology. Moreover, from what source does Marx obtain information about the ultimate goal of history? Who gave Marx the secret to the "riddle"? With respect to the promised benefits of communism, are they worth the price in murder and human sacrifice that must be paid?

If we search in the writings of Marx for reflection on these problems, we find only the imperative that we stop our questioning, for our questions are "abstractions." This occlusion of questions which might forestall the atheist humanist's desire to destroy the world so that he can build it anew in his own image is equivalent to the magical occlusion of man's creaturely status by the Gnostics and Renaissance Hermeticists. All allowed a vision of transfigured reality to block out the reality of creaturely being. Because of the depth of this disease of the spirit, it presents to public order in the modern world the supreme challenge of disease of the soul impermeable to rational argument.

3.

The Enlightenment's Dead End

"Modern" men of the 17th century were "enlightened" by interest in "science." We 21st-century beneficiaries of modern science may not understand how the Enlightenment's pursuit of "science" rejected noetic reason of classical philosophy. These good and bad aspects of the Enlightenment had an impact on the founding documents of the American regime.

Enlightenment concepts like "law of nature" and "natural rights" conveyed meanings far different from classical concepts of "natural law" and "right by nature." And the Enlightenment view of man was quite different from orthodox Christian tradition. As we saw in this passage from Francis Yates' study of Giordano Bruno,

"What has changed is Man, now no longer only the pious spectator of God's wonders in the creation, and worshipper of God himself above the creation, but Man the operator, Man who seeks to draw power from the divine and natural order."[1]

Who were these Enlightenment thinkers and what did they offer? As we shall see in Chapter 8, Allan Bloom believed that the "Enlightenment was the first philosophically inspired 'movement,' a theoretical school that is a political force at the same time."[2] The pursuit of truth which is the hallmark of classical philosophy now was replaced by the pursuit of power. Before the Enlightenment, philosophers contemplated nature. Now they sought to control it. Bloom identifies Machiavelli as one of these thinkers, but Machia-

---

[1] Frances Yates, *Giordano Bruno and the Hermetic Tradition* (Chicago: University of Chicago Press, 1964), 212.

[2] Allan Bloom, *The Closing of the American Mind* (Simon and Schuster: New York, 1987), 262.

velli is more often cited as representative of the Renaissance. Still, what was "new" in the Renaissance was continued in "modern" Enlightenment ideas.

Ephraim Emerton defined the Renaissance as "the new birth throughout the regions of Latin civilization of an interest in classical study, no longer merely as a means to the end of a better understanding of the Christian writers or as a preparation to become a clergyman but as a means of personal culture."[3] Conveyed in this definition is a sense of curiosity, of individual self-assertion, in opposition to the medieval virtues of self-denial and renunciation of the world. In literature, this is visible in the new use of the vernacular for the expression of personal and national feeling, whereas the common tongue had previously been discredited as a medium for the expression of serious ideas.

Though the creators of Gothic architecture are anonymous, Petrarch (1304-1374) declared fame to be the proper object of human desire[4] and revised the traditional Christian valuation of history. Where heretofore Christ was the focus of history, now Petrarch saw the conversion of Rome to Christianity as the dark age and the period of pre-Christian Rome as an age of light and glory.[5] At the same time, vows which Christian nobles were inclined to make, imposing onerous tasks upon themselves and their clients for the glory of God, faded from the scene.[6] Literary reflections on death, which previously had singularly pious functions, now came to express a secular emotion only. In addition, the rise of numerology, magic and astrology, pseudo-sciences which promised knowledge and control of divine forces, tended to replace religious piety.

---

[3] Ephraim Emerton, *The Beginnings of Modern Europe, 1250-1450* (Boston: Ginn and Co.,1917), 464.

[4] Ibid., 480.

[5] Erwin Panofsky, *Renaissance and Renascences in Western Art* (New York: Harper & Row, Publishers, Icon Editions, 1972), 10.

[6] J. Huizinga, *The Waning of the Middle Ages: A Study of the Thought and Art in France and the Netherlands in the XIVth and XVth Centuries* (London: Edward Arnold & Co., 1937), 80.

The Renaissance also represented major changes in people's moral and worldly attitudes. "By the mid- fifteenth century the family man, the magistrate, the soldier, might hold up his head. The monk no longer monopolized virtue. The stock sermon topic, whether a merchant or a soldier was more certain of damnation, lost its sting, though it continued to be preached."[7]

Along with the elevation of secular pursuits, there occurred a change in the nature of documentation. Thus, writes Denys Hay, "after the early years of the fifteenth century the monastic chronicle dried up, even in France and England; elsewhere it had become parochial long before."[8] In place of chronicles, the historical record is to be found in the writings of lay administrators and the records of diplomatic agents. In turn, the nobility developed what in effect was its own civil service composed of lay, as opposed to clerical, secretaries.[9] "Man" as the "operator," was a view which Thomas Hobbes (1588-1679) shared with Machiavelli and the new physical scientists of the then "modern" era. Francis Bacon (1561-1626), in his "Great Instauration," expressed in a similar fashion the need to act on, or operate upon, the world, rather than to be content with contemplation of its grandeur.

By advocating a new science which would displace the Scholastic method, Bacon expressed an antagonism, shared by virtually every modern thinker, to propositional reasoning which had dominated education of the Medieval schools since the 13th century. The mechanistic models of this new science seemed like a breath of fresh air to these students faced with continual drilling in what had certainly become third-rate handbooks of Scholasticism. Rene Descartes (1596-1650) succinctly described this antagonism when he wrote in his "Discourse on Method" that Scholastic philosophy is

---

[7] Denys Hay, *The Italian Renaissance in its Historical Background* (Cambridge: At The University Press, 1961), 126.

[8] Denys Hay, *Europe in the Fourteenth and Fifteenth Centuries* (New York: Holt, Rinehart and Winston, Inc., 1966), 3.

[9] Ibid, 7.

most convenient for those who have only very mediocre minds; for the obscurity of the distinctions and principles which they use enables them to speak about all things as boldly as if they really knew them, and to maintain everything they say against the subtlest and most skillful, without anyone being able to convince them of their error.[10] In this spirit of utter rejection of philosophy of the Medieval schools, both Bacon and Descartes constructed new intellectual methods.

The political science of Thomas Hobbes, John Locke and Jean-Jacques Rousseau is the full outgrowth of these new scientific inquiries.[11] They are commonly called "Social Contract" theorists and their concepts of the origins of society, power, law, and rights shaped the Framers' understanding of politics and their role as statesmen. Unfortunately, though convenient for the movement toward independence of the British colonies in America from the British Crown, Social Contract political theory is not philosophically sound. In other words, the Framers utilized ideas that would come back later to threaten destruction of civil society in the American democratic republic.

---

[10] Rene Descartes, *Descartes. Discourse on Method and Other Writings,* E.E. Sutcliffe, trans. (Baltimore, Penguin Books, (1968), "Discourse on the Method of Property Conducting One's Reason and of Seeking the Truth in the Sciences," 85. For a full examination of the rejection of dogmatic philosophy, see Basil Willey, *The Seventeenth Century Background: Studies in the Thought of the Age in Relation to Poetry and Religion,* reprint of 1934 ed. (London: Chatto and Windus, 1962), 1-23.

[11] This 'interpretation' is disputed by Leo Strauss, who taught that the real basis of Hobbes' political philosophy is not modern science but his perception of "human life." See Leo Strauss, *The Political Philosophy of Hobbes: Its Basis and Its Genesis,* Elsa M. Sinclair, trans. (Chicago: University of Chicago Press, Phoenix Books, 1963). The more traditional view is expressed by Michael Oakeshott in "Introduction to *Leviathan,*" *Hobbes on Civil Association* (Berkeley and Los Angeles: University of California Press, 1975), 1-74.

Thomas Hobbes

Thomas Hobbes lived during the period of the Puritan Revolution. England suffered the worst political crisis its history; politics had ceased and civil war wracked the country. The theory of political order he formulated, therefore, struck at what appeared to him to be the main cause of these disorders—religious claims to higher authority than the sovereign. Hobbes' answer to such disorders of his day was to develop a concept of order that completely removed all religious elements from politics and only treated the "true" reality that motivates political action—power. As such, Hobbes' *Leviathan* is a masterpiece of analysis of the lust for power, a demonic element in man, and the consequences that follow for politics.

Hobbes, seeing that political order was being destroyed by a war between Puritan fanatics and defenders *of* the British monarchy, sought to expel completely the Christian God from politics. For Hobbes the "body politic" was not a community of souls participating in the life of God, but is literally "bodies in motion." Though Hobbes was truly concerned with physical bodies in motion, both natural bodies and political bodies, his Leviathan is based upon *ideas* of bodies. These are not innate ideas impressed on our souls by a beneficent God before we were born, but originate in our senses.

Upon this empiricism, Hobbes built his entire political edifice. The knowledge which man has of reality originates in the senses. But what is primary, what we really know are the ideas in our mind, the concepts we formulate by reasoning to order our senses. All that we know is in the names we use; so Hobbes begins with the definition of the names he will use in the construction of this geometrical edifice of political order and builds his own made-to-order reality. From this he deduced the following:

a) Man is not social. He is a-social and acquisitive.
b) Man is not motivated by a highest good (*summum bonum*) but by *summum malum,* the fear of death.

c) Community is the artifice of man's reason, formulated by attention to the "laws of nature."

d) By "reason," Hobbes means discursive "reason," our ability to calculate.

e) "Laws of nature" are not "Nature's Laws." They are theorems that can be deduced from the careful and systematic definition of names.

f) Man's natural right is a "license" or power to seek one's interest.

g) The order of the animal community is the order of man.

Though Hobbes' political theory shocked the sentiment of English society, as well it should, John Locke's political philosophy is not much better.

John Locke

"Reason," for John Locke, too, is not the *nous* of Anaximander or Plato. Locke's reason "is nothing else but the faculty of deducing unknown truths from principles or propositions that are already known."[12] How then does he reconcile this concept of reason with concepts of right, justice and the good of classical philosophy? What of the great moral categories of good and evil? Locke's complete reply, one derived from his *Essay Concerning Human Understanding* (1690) and his early *Essays on the Law of Nature* (1660), is three-fold:

a) good and evil are functions of pleasure or pain;

b) moral good and evil, justice and injustice, are determined by law or some rule enforced by a common sovereign; and

---

[12] John Locke, *An Essay Concerning Human Understanding,* Alexander Fraser, ed., 2 vols. (New York: Dover Publications, Inc., 1959), L 1.9.

    c) there are universal laws of nature which govern the behavior
    of men, but these laws are discovered in sense-experience.
The famous passage in which Locke reduces good and evil to sense
experience states:

> Things then are good or evil, only in reference to pleasure or
> pain. That we call good, which is apt to cause or increase pleas-
> ure, or diminish pain in us; or else to procure or preserve us the
> possession of any other good or absence of evil. And, on the
> contrary, we name that evil, which is apt to produce or increase
> any pain, or diminish any pleasure in us: or else to procure us
> any evil, or deprive us of any good.[13]

Locke implies that there is no justice or right by nature, in the
sense in which Plato, Aristotle or Cicero saw it. "Virtue and vice are
names pretended and supposed everywhere to stand for actions in
their own nature right and wrong."[14] It is obvious that, to Locke,
virtue and vice are "attributed only to such actions as in each country and society are in reputation and discredit,"[15] *i.e.,* right and
wrong are what the dominant powers say they are. We must keep
this in mind when we examine the "the laws of nature" and
"rights" prominently proclaimed in the Declaration of Independence. Some interpret these concepts from the natural law tradition.
We think that a closer examination of Thomas Jefferson's draft of
the Declaration reveals a more Lockean and Hobbesian view.

    Locke argued that underlying civil law and custom is only the
supposition, not certain knowledge, that what in fact is declared
unjust really is wrong. Yet, peculiarly, Locke was certain that an ethics based on analysis of sense experience and reflection was as secure a moral philosophy as one could desire.

    Locke thought that ethics was a subject capable of as much

---

[13] John Locke, *An Essay Concerning Human Understanding, 11.20.2.*
[14] Ibid., II.28.10.
[15] Ibid., II.28.10.

demonstration and clarity as geometry. Of course, Locke says, there is the problem that moral ideas are more complex than those of the figures used in mathematics. But this complexity can be overcome by "definitions, setting down that collection of simple ideas, which every term shall stand for; and then using the terms steadily and constantly for the precise collection."[16] Moral ideas when traced ultimately to pleasure and pain do not convey the sense of universal moral obligation that is the chief strength of natural law. Perhaps sensing this rhetorical weakness in his construction, Locke developed his concept of the laws of nature. He deduced that there are laws of nature from the fact that people contend so much about the problem of what is right universally. Without the law of nature, without an absolute "eternal" principle of moral good, "everything would have to depend on human will.[17]

That there is a law of nature, Locke was convinced because it is necessary lest what is right be simply the will of the stronger. Within this philosophically limited perspective, Locke argues that since our senses indicate God's existence, so it must follow that the world has some purpose. "God intends man to do something."[18] And we are morally bound by that intention of God to certain classes of action. We are bound not to do those things which are completely forbidden, we are bound to "maintain certain sentiments, such as reverence and fear of the Deity,"[19] and we are bound to acts of charity and prudence.

Locke's *Second Treatise of Government,* written between 1676 and 1682, also presents grave difficulties. It lacks rigorous argument and does not defend the assumptions and concepts upon which it is based, concepts such as the law of nature, state of nature, and the social contract.

Because Locke's analysis of human nature and community is

---

[16] Ibid., *IV.3.25.*

[17] John Locke, *Essays on the Law of Nature,* W. von Leyden, ed. (Oxford: At the Clarendon Press, 1951), I15-121.

[18] Ibid., 125.

[19] Ibid.

restricted to the passionate level where man seeks advantage and convenience, he defines the best ruler as the prince who aids the acquisition of property and its right use. Such a prince, Locke says, is "godlike."[20] Property was broadly defined by Locke to include life, liberty, and estate. As such, it conveys a sense of the purposes of life, as Locke saw them. The law of nature was the rational rule by which man lived out his life within life's overarching acquisitive purposes. The law of nature "obliges every one: And Reason, which is that Law, teaches all Mankind, who will but consult it, that being all equal and independent, no one ought to harm another in his Life, Health, Liberty, or Possessions."[21]

The origin of property is in labor, and this labor by which something external is taken and made one's own is a law of nature.[22] The law of nature favors men who are acquisitive, rational, and industrious creatures, just as God prefers men such as these over those who are quarrelsome and contentious. Here, too, Locke ignored the insight of Classical philosophy that the common good is knowable only to the good man, whose judgment is the standard and measure of what is right by nature for himself and for the community of men. Because Locke has no equivalent view of the best man, he is reduced to perceiving justice and the common good in terms of property and of the property owner who is a good citizen because he rationally calculates his private pleasure and pain.

Unlike Hobbes who viewed man In the state of nature as a-social, Locke assumes that man is a social creature, but not a "political" creature. Like all Social Contract thinkers, John Locke was persuaded that "the political" was not an essential attribute of man. He disagreed with Aristotle that man is a political being. What is

---

[20] Peter Laslett, *John Locke, Two Treatises of Government* (Cambridge: At The University Press, 1963), 42. Pagination is cited by paragraph from the Laslett edition.

[21] Ibid., 6.

[22] Ibid., 30-1.

political, for Locke, is an accident, an artifice. This meant, among other things, that Locke and the Social Contract thinkers abandoned the Classical philosophic inquiry into political order that is best by nature. No political rule can be best by nature, because nature is pre-political.

This was the perfect credo for Locke's times and in practical terms inspired those who sought to justify revolution. If political existence is the artifice of those ruled, and not the dominion of the anointed of God, then government originates in the very ones who are ruled. If the limits they set for government are broken, then they may just take that dominion away and give it to another, someone who will follow their dictates. These words of Locke spoke to a new man, becoming dominant in the late 17th century, new men who would give up their quest of heaven in exchange for a heavenly world.

England at the time Locke wrote his *Second Treatise of Government* was much like a small town after a revival meeting. Exhausted from excesses of spiritual enthusiasms, and with visions of a New Jerusalem now past, Englishmen were ready to settle down to the less spiritually tiring, but more pleasurable fare of business as usual. Locke's *Second Treatise* captured this exhaustion of the soul in English culture and gave it a political credo by which to live. English colonists in 18th-century America knew a good thing when they saw it, and John Locke became the patron saint of the American revolution. But revolutions do not stop where we want them and in France during the reign of Louis XVI, the revolution took a new turn toward violence and terror.

Jean-Jacques Rousseau

The influence of Jean-Jacques Rousseau (1712-1778) upon the great political events of the eighteenth century, especially the American and French Revolutions, should not be underestimated. His concepts inspired such disparate democratic activists as James Madison, Thomas Jefferson, Robespierre, and Saint-Just and were the epitome of *esprit revolutionaire* that engaged Tocqueville to admire the non-revolutionary democracy in America.

As we will see in Chapter 8, three 19th-century Spanish traditionalists, Juan Donoso Cortés, the Catholic priest, Jaime Balmes, and the scholar and literary historian, Marcelino Menéndez Pelayo, saw Rousseau as the originator of a revolutionary ideology carried to Spain when Napoleon invaded the Iberian Peninsula in 1808. Turning Spain against that ideology, they believed, was necessary, if traditional order in Spain was to survive the viruses of modern ideology.

Snuggled into the first paragraph of Chapter One of Rousseau's *Social Contract* (1762) are the seeds of a revolution against government and traditional order. Man was born free, but is everywhere in bondage. This or that man believes himself the master of his fellow men, but is nevertheless more of a slave than they. How did this change from freedom into bondage come about? I do not know. Under what conditions can it be rendered legitimate? This problem I believe I can solve.[23]

Rousseau is asserting that all the accoutrements of social power are illegitimate. That is, of course, a tremendous indictment of political order and conveys a spirit which roiled Europe during the 18th century, the spirit of resentment, of injury, and rebellion. Rousseau's Social Contract reveals a will to reconstitute society anew, a revolutionary will which he indicates is motivated by a desire for freedom that will not hesitate to force men to be free.

If that is our condition, how do we overcome a condition of slavery, of bondage, and become free? Rousseau answered by turning to a "social contract." By coming together in a collective association and compacting to create a greater community, a collective moral body is created which "will defend and protect with all the collective might, the person and property of each associate, and in

---

[23] Jean-Jacques Rousseau, *The Social Contract*, Willmoore Kendall, trans. (Chicago: Henry Regnery Co., Gateway Edition, 1954), 2.

virtue of which each associate, though he becomes a member of the group, nevertheless obeys only himself, and remains as free as before."[24] But man does not really remain as free as before because he is now obliged to other men who are his fellow citizens, and to the sovereign, the General Will. Moreover, man's freedom has changed qualitatively. Man's actions now have a moral significance.

Our contemporary notion of participatory democracy, now assisted by communication technology that permits direct decision-making by members of a community, conveys the sense of Rousseau's reasoning in the *Social Contract*. That by willing man's actions now have a moral significance is a particularly important concept. All of us are moral agents, not by virtue of our having created or given consent to laws by which we are organized in civil society, but because our acts are intrinsically rational, that is, they are. to the extent they are guided by reason, moral acts. In this sense, a morally rational act is one which is limited not merely by our own consent, but by justice open to the divine. That is the importance of the concept of "natural law" espoused by Cicero. What limits our acts and thus gives them rationality is an unchangeable ontological relationship of our acts to justice rooted in nature.

Rousseau, however, is saying the opposite, that only we ourselves determine the morality and rationality, the limitations of our own acts, by consenting to the laws which bind us in civil society. If we do not have that opportunity, then we are not really men, because for Rousseau, to be human means to be participants in a social contract. To be morally meaningful, our actions must be preceded by a conscious act of assent to the laws that bind us in civil society. So long as the sovereign can be understood to have been created by the willful act of the citizens and serves as the representative of the General Will we are free from bondage. Rousseau's political system places no limitations upon the sovereign, however. If morality is actualized only by obedience to self-imposed law, then all concepts of government limited by what is right by nature

---

[24] Ibid., 18.

or eternal justice have been thrown to the wind.

Rousseau has removed the great limitations imposed upon government by the Western philosophical tradition and has, by attempting to elevate man, created what Hobbes directly sought, the omnipotent state, what Hobbes called a *Leviathan*. That explains why Rousseau addresses himself to those recalcitrant few who may not wish to be free in the sense in which he has defined freedom. Whoever refuses to obey the general will shall be constrained to do so by the entire body politic, which is only another way of saying that his fellows shall force him to be free.[25]

Because of such passages, and the general structure of his political system, Rousseau has been called a "totalitarian democrat."[26] In Rousseau's *Social Contract* of 1762, we can find the concepts necessary for totalitarian democracy. The name, totalitarian democrat, is paradoxical because a democrat is supposed to honor freedom, while a totalitarian honors it not at all. An examination of Rousseau's concept of the General Will gets us a bit closer to understanding what he means and how dangerous such Enlightenment concepts can be.

Rousseau specifically tells us that no particular interest, however many may share it, can be a general interest. The will of the individual "tends by its very nature toward partiality-8 whereas the General Will tends toward equality. "A *given will is* either general or it is not."[27] Is the General Will the will of the whole people? Yes, Rousseau answers, but only so long as the will of the whole people is general. His argument goes like this:

a)   The General Will is always well-intentioned;

---

[25] Ibid., 25.

[26] The best study of the origins of totalitarianism in democratic theory is J.L. Talmon, *The Origins Of Totalitarian Democracy* (New York: Frederick A. Praeger, 1960).

[27] Rousseau, *The Social Contract,* 15.

b) The people's deliberations, however, are not always what they ought to be;

c) "the will of everybody" is different from the General Will;[28]

d) "The people is never corrupted, but is frequently misinformed."[29]

e) A will need not be unanimous in order for it to be general; what is necessary is that every voice be taken into account.

To ask if there is such a substance as the General Will misses the insight that Rousseau's political philosophy is not based in reality, it is the figment of Rousseau's bountiful imagination. Here the problem becomes complicated because some important scholars, like the English philosopher Thomas Hill Green (1836-1882), associated Rousseau's General Will with the concept of the Good or of divine *nous* in Classical Greek philosophy.[30] There is no basis for such a conclusion.

Reality, that which is, in ancient Greek philosophers is a hierarchy of goods which proceeds from the ultimate divine good which is beyond being. Noetic experience of this divine *nous* orders man's understanding of what is good action and becomes socially effective through the influence of men recognized for their noetic faculties. A constitution in this classical sense was better or worse to the degree that its laws manifested *nous*.

Rousseau, however, sees "will" as the legitimizing source of public order. Whereas what is good is a matter of rational public debate by men who have *nous*, Rousseau's concept of the General

---

[28] Ibid., 38.

[29] Ibid.

[30] See Thomas Hill Green, *Lectures on the Principles of Political* Obligation (Ann Arbor: University of Michigan Press, Ann Arbor Paperbacks, 1967), par. 68 and Richard Bishirjian, "Thomas Hill Green's Political Philosophy," *Political Science Reviewer*, Fall 1974, Vol. 4. No 1.

Will thrusts public debate along the lines of a search for the generality of will, which because it lacks specificity would likewise preclude the search for the good. The more removed from the specific, the historical, the concrete, the more general or abstract it becomes, the less claim to rightness does any moral judgment have. And yet it is the moral legitimacy of a community which actualizes the General Will that gives it importance for Rousseau.

Clearly, we are dealing in Rousseau with a new type of political theory, not a mere adjustment of classical or Christian concepts to the problems of a new era. For example, the interesting substance which Rousseau calls the General Will is sometimes unenlightened. When the General Will takes a particular object, for example, it ceases to be the General Will. It is but a product of the people, and the people are often misinformed.

We have already seen indications of a revolutionary political potential in Rousseau's thought, what can be called the experience of revolt, of a new view of human nature which sees man as making his own moral nature by collective action, and a new emphasis on procedures and participation in government as the means by which to resolve substantive problems of political order. But, in the concept of General Will we see a displacement of a view of order, oriented toward the divine, which judges public policy on the basis of whether or not it serves a knowable common good or interest.

Public policy analysis in the Classical tradition, which consists of prudential analysis of public action, assumes the need for governors who seek the good in community life. Political community is something natural. It exists not by the will of human beings but because human beings experience it as existing in tension or openness to a good beyond itself. Rousseau, however, has argued that a community is defined only by its own self-willing. The limits upon political community are immanent—within the community. Rousseau's civil society is a wholly self-contained polity guided by immanent ends which are discoverable in a fictitious General Will, not in the structure of being, of nature, and community.

We have, then, a dynamic, aggressive, constantly self-aggrandizing sense of political community, the proto-type of the "Great Society," or worse, a "Fatherland" affirmed by national ambitions, but there is very little in Rousseau's concept that would yield a view of the "Good Society" or the "best" political community by nature.

Because life in such a community is not lived according to deliberation concerning what is right by nature, Rousseau develops his concept of a "Legislator." The General Will must be brought to see things as they are, for though it wills the right road, it must be shown the way. There emerges, then, the need for a Legislator. The Legislator, Rousseau argued has a mind of the highest order (much like his own, we could observe) capable of discovering the best laws for each nation. This mind, he said, must have an insight into every human passion, but not be affected by any. Rousseau is obviously thinking of a superhuman mind and he says as much.

The Legislator must feel within himself the capacity to change human nature. "He must, in a word, initially strip each man of the resources that are his and his alone, in order to give him new resources that are foreign to his nature, and that he can utilize only with the help of others."[31] The emphasis of classical philosophy upon actualizing one's nature or potential as a man by right action gives place in Rousseau to a need for a legislator who will impose that "nature," now conceived as arbitrarily chosen patterns of behavior, on unwilling men.

In intellectual history, as we saw in Chapter 3, Rousseau's view of a Legislator is a step in a general development which begins in Renaissance Hermeticism, leads through Kant and Hegel, and culminates in Nietzsche's concept of the *Übermensch*, or superman. Rousseau's Legislator, then, is not really a man. Rousseau is not speaking of the common practice of attributing fanciful dimensions to founders of nations or great political leaders. Rousseau is actually arguing that at those great moments when political communities are formed and dynasties are created, it is not men who are necessary

---

[31] Rousseau, *The Social Contract*, 58.

for the task, but god-men.

And there it is again, just as Locke asserted that the prince is god-like. In the case of 17th-century England, to be like a god was foundational to Hermetic "magic" and a part of the vernacular of a culture seeking to break the bonds of orthodox Christianity. Who, after all, can strip man of his resources and give him new ones? The problem with this view is that man, even the Legislator, is not God. And when men aspire to be gods, they destroy their humanity.

In the 20th century, the consequence of the aspiration to be God led to totalitarianism. This aspiration requires the total removal of all limits to human rationality, the search for the common good in politics and the unlimited, total use of political power for the accomplishment of ends that cannot be achieved on this earth. If man has no abiding nature, then man's nature can be shaped or made in conformance with totalitarian rules.

To assure that his project was actualized, Rousseau, like Machiavelli, Hobbes, and Locke, advocated the necessity of civil religion. Their reasons were not exactly similar, but together they constitute a formidable assessment of the fragility of modern communal existence and the need for the state as the single most powerful means by which the political body coheres.

How can a community of wholly appetitive, economic men hold together, if no common bond except the social contract or passion connects them in political community? If men can no longer depend upon sacred traditions to ameliorate the contradictions of existence, then sacred traditions must be fabricated anew.

Rousseau's solution is civil religion. Civil religion is efficacious, he argued, because it sees no disjunction between positive and divine law and "makes the fatherland the object of the citizens' adoration, and so teaches them that service to the state and service to the state's tutelary deity are one and the same thing."[32]

For Rousseau, the sovereign establishes the dogmas of civil reli-

---

[32] Ibid., 213.

gion. These would not be, strictly speaking, dogmas of a religious character, but rather sentiments for participation in society, i.e., sentiments without which no man can be either a good citizen or a loyal subject.[33] Those who do not believe in this dogma can be banished on the grounds of a basic lack of sociability. The primacy of unity in Rousseau's theory, coupled with his postulate of a civil religion, displaces the primacy of truth. The truth of the laws, their justice, is not a consideration. What is of value is its power to contribute to social unity. Rousseau's civil religion, therefore, brings to the fore a central disagreement between the Enlightenment and traditional order and assists in our discovery of answers to the question, "Can this country be saved?"

"Tradition" values political order attuned to existence-in-truth. The goods which hold men together in political community are understood to be rooted in experience of a higher order, a commonly shared experience of justice, right, and the common good. The political theory of the Enlightenment, however, unable to accept the reality of transcendent order, is compelled to assert the primacy of autonomous unity made possible by civil religion transparent only to the immediate needs of maintaining the communal bond. We call such a conception of political community as described here, "The Enlightenment's Dead End."

This discussion would not be necessary were it not for the influence of the Enlightenment on the education and works of the Framers of the Constitution of the United States. American democracy generates demands for "equality" and the actualization of "natural rights." The subtle difference between a view of man as made in the image of God and "equality" of condition and natural law and natural rights defines the confusion imposed on contemporary American culture by the Enlightenment.

---

[33] Ibid., 220.

4.

Esprit Revolutionaire

"Modern" men of the 17th century were "enlightened" by interest in "science." We 21st-century beneficiaries of modern science may not understand that this Enlightenment pursuit of "science" had negative aspects when that science rejected noetic reason or *nous* of classical philosophy. These positive and negative aspects of Enlightenment "science" had an impact on the founding documents of American government.

Enlightenment concepts like "law of nature" and "natural rights" conveyed meanings far different from the classical concepts of "natural law" and "right by nature," so Enlightenment thinkers, the *philosophes*, had a different view of man, political order, and history than their classical counterparts. In order to examine the character of their intellectual concepts, we must visit the ideas that shaped the "political religion" of 18th-century revolutionary France, which brought the French *philosophes* to reject traditional order, and 19th-century German idealism.

In the first case, the French *philosophes* infused the French Revolution and the killing fields of 18th-century France with *esprit revolutionaire*, the spirit of revolution. That spirit is key to understanding Tocqueville's search for the reasons behind the stability of American democracy as he articulated in his *Democracy in America*. In order to get a fuller sense of what Tocqueville meant, we must begin by taking a look at what he called "a new kind of religion," or what Destutt De Tracy and Napoleon Bonaparte called "ideology."[1]

Barry Cooper, a University of Calgary political theorist, explains that if it is the law of nature and human progress to eliminate pre-

---

[1] Here I follow my mentor at Notre Dame, Gerhart Niemeyer, whose *Between Nothingness and Paradise* contains a rigorous analysis of an ideological style that he calls the "total critique of reality."

judice and everything that is harmful, nature and history require that ever new prejudices and things that are harmful be disposed of.[2] Referring to Hannah Arendt, Cooper explains that ideologies are "isms" that "to the satisfaction of their adherents can explain everything and every occurrence by deducing it from a single presence."[3] Ideology is a replacement or counter to reality because there is no reality to which the "idea" of ideology refers. Ideology does not refer to anything real. The concept of ideology, therefore, must be understood as "the logic of an idea" that somehow, by an act of human imagination, is applied to historical events. Because the French "ideologues" rejected reality as it is given in existence, their *esprit revolutionaire* had very grave consequences.

Destutt DeTracy (1754–1836)

The first person to make use of the concept "ideology." His work on ideology, entitled *Eléments d'idéologie*, viewed ideology as the "science of ideas." The "Enlightenment" notion that there is a "science of ideas" evokes a sense of true knowledge, "science," that is certifiable because it is based in "reason" and the physical sciences. "Reason" to the ideologues was ratiocination and based in sense experience. They were critical of Napoleon who responded by calling them "Ideologues." By that Napoleon meant that they were "dreamers."

France in the 18th-century had many "ideologues," but they were not mere dreamers. They shared ideas and attitudes that were later recognized aspects of totalitarian movements of the 20th century—collectively they rejected existence, found reality itself to be defective, and sought to replace it with a different, better order than that given in reality and based on their own speculations.

---

[2] Barry Cooper, *New Political Religions or An Analysis of Modern Terrorism* (Columbia: University of Missouri Press, 2004), 12.

[3] Ibid., 13.

Jean Meslier[4] (1664–1729)

A French Catholic priest who disguised his atheism and developed an argument for total rejection of society. In his "Testament," which came to light after his death, Meslier denounced religion and philosophy, arguing that the existence of God was incompatible with the existence of evil and that Christianity legitimated suffering and submission to tyranny. Meslier hoped his ideas would incite an insurrection against the rich, high placed, and powerful. Long before Nietzsche, Meslier committed himself to the destruction of God and, before Marx, Meslier saw communism as the natural order of human life.

Étienne-Gabriel Morelly[5] (1717–1778)

A contemporary of Rousseau known for two works attributed to him—a poem entitled "Basiliade" and a philosophical work entitled *Code de la Nature*, which interprets the poem. "Basiliade" describes two kingdoms, one that is the embodiment of Nature and Truth and another where Interest, Error, and Falsehood are dominant. The latter (Error and Falsehood) is symbolic of order as man has known it for millennia. This historical world is the creation of an evil demiurge and as such the world is an alien power.

As we have seen, this type of radical dualism is similar in ancient Gnosticism. Ancient Gnostics thought that the world was created by an evil being who trapped the divine spark of God in material nature. That spark could only be released by knowledge (gnosis) which the Gnostics claimed to possess. The "gnosis" or knowledge that releases man from evil, according to Meslier, is knowledge of the order of nature. For Morelly, unfortunately, historical society and property is the material form of man's rebellion against nature, and Morelly proposed that property should be eliminated. He wrote, "Nothing in society will belong to anyone, either

---

[4] Gerhart Niemeyer, *Between Nothingness and Paradise* (Baton Rouge, LA: Louisiana State University, 1971), 6-17.

[5] Ibid., 17-29.

as a personal possession or as capital goods, except the things for which the person has immediate use, for either his needs, his pleasures, or his daily work."

Gabriel Bonnot de Mably[6] (1709–1785)

Also advocated the abolition of private property, was critical of inherited wealth and privilege of the nobility, and fashioned a concept of equality based on distribution of wealth according to needs. For Mably, the natural order was an egalitarian socialist community.

Jean-Jacques Rousseau (1712–1778)

By far a more gifted theorist than these others, who, nonetheless, shared similar views. Rousseau wrote that the introduction of property led to slavery and misery. The current historical era in which he lived was one in which "Man was born free, but is everywhere in bondage." Rousseau addresses this historical problem in his *Social Contract* by creating a system in which man moves from a state of nature into membership of a group in which, nevertheless, man obeys only himself and remains as free as before.

Rousseau admits that the State of Nature is sheer speculation, essentially an illusion, but it is a necessary hypothesis in order to overcome the slavery of mankind. There are other elements in Rousseau's *Social Contract*—the Legislator and his call for a civil religion—that has led scholars to suggest that Rousseau yielded to what they call, "the totalitarian temptation."[7] In totalitarian movements, such "banishment" is a way to identify specific classes as enemies. *Former People: The Final Days of the Russian Aristocracy* by Douglas Smith[8] explains what happened to aristocrats who became class enemies in Soviet Russia.

---

[6] Ibid., 29-36.

[7] J. L. Talmon, *Origins of Totalitarian Democracy*, 3rd ed. (New York: W. W. Norton, 2010).

[8] Picador; Reprint edition (September 24, 2013).

Marquis de Condorcet[9] (1743 –1794)

Condorcet is important because in *Outlines of an Historical View of the Progress of the Human Mind* he introduces a philosophy of history. Condorcet sees human knowledge as the product of sense experience, pleasure, and pain, which progresses through ten epochs of history overcoming at each stage prejudice and ultimately reaching a condition of enlightenment. Condorcet believed that his own thought was the end of history.

During the sixty-six years from the death of Meslier in 1729 to the posthumous publication of Condorcet's history of the progress of the human mind in 1795, an *esprit revolutionaire* had a dominant influence on French intellectual culture and events in France. That *esprit revolutionaire* rejected society as it was received, blamed property for human misery, and led inescapably to revolution as a way to achieve a better, "natural," order. During the French Revolution killing was justified in order to attain that better order. The history of the French Revolution explains what can happen when consciousness of the basis of order is lost and traditions, institutions, and human beings are sacrificed to an imaginary substitute reality.

[9] Op. cit., 44-49.

5.

Instability of Democracy

The instability that Americans and Western Europeans are experiencing in their politics is due to three old, and one new, feature of democratic regimes.

a) First, democracies tend to lead to demands for equality. That is a demand incapable of being reconciled because citizens are by nature unequal.

b) Second, democracies favor extreme calls for freedom and liberty that cannot be reconciled with the necessities of political order.

c) Third, democracies deter the best and the brightest from seeking elective office and tend to elevate the less gifted, or morally callous, to positions of political leadership.

d) To these three, we must add a fourth feature, that of "Celebrity." Persons who are known for their "knownness" have become attractive candidates for high office.

Are we living in an age in which "celebrity" has become a criterion for election for public office? If so, what place is there in American democracy for qualified citizens who are non-celebrities?

How the rise of a celebrity culture came about was first examined in 1961 by Daniel Boorstin in *The Image or What Happened to the American Dream*. In a distinguished career, Boorstin was Librarian of Congress from 1975 to 1987, professor of history at the University of Chicago, and author of a three volume study of America: Vol. I, *The Americans: the Colonial Experience* (1964), Vol. 2, *The National Experience (1967)* and Vol. 3, *The Democratic Experience* (1974).

In some ways, *The Image or What Happened to the American Dream* can be viewed as the first in this series of studies of America. Boorstin writes that "since about 1900, we seem to have discovered the processes by which fame is manufactured."[1] Since the turn of the last century, an increasing proportion of our experience consists of pseudo-events. Boorstin defines "psudeo-events" as "an ambiguous truth" (23). Examples of a pseudo-event are "Quiz Shows," "elaborately contrived situations that purported to inform the public" (41). Our experience is directed toward performance, not content. That explains why surveys of the 1960 Presidential Debate showed that John F. Kennedy won the televised version of the debate but Richard Nixon won the radio broadcast version of the debate.

There are also substantive changes that have occurred to reshape how we experience reality. Boorstin calls them the "dissolution of forms" (133-139). In literature the formal structure of the literary form, language, rhetoric, vocabulary, and dramatic structure are inseparable from idea. With the introduction of "Abridged Books," all of that has been excised and only the ghost of formal reality remains (149). In short, "[t]he shadow has become the substance" (133). These substance-less shadows may be seen in the introduction of motion pictures. "Stars" were manufactured and made distinguishable from actors by their "well-knownness" (154). The "Star" became what Boorstin called a pseudo-event, "a definable publicizable personality (156). Even universities became celebrities, known for their "well- knownness" (168). As we have seen, some parents will do anything to get their "students" admitted to "name" colleges and universities, thus forgetting that the purpose of those institutions is "education." And works of art came to be valued by how widely they were reproduced (126).

All this changed our consciousness of our own selves: our personality became "the attention-getting image of ourselves, our image of our own behavior" (202). If the era of celebrity in which we

---

[1] Daniel J. Boorstin, *The Image: A Guide to Pseudo-Events in America* (Atheneum, New York, 1987) originally published in 1961 as *The Image or What Hppened to the American Dream*. All page references cited in the body of this text are from the Atheneum (Vintage paperback) edition.

live is one where "the shadow has become the substance" (204), we must ask whether our politicians are the source of the disorders of this era or the American people who elected them.

For that reason, we turn our attention to Alexis de Tocqueville who in *Democracy in America* raised important questions about democracy in France and in America. Among the issues that concerned Tocqueville are six that contribute to the fragility of civil society in which we find ourselves.

1) The attack on traditional order in 18th-century France by the French *philosophes* and Enlightenment ideas that guided our Founding Fathers when it came time to fashion a government for a new nation;

2) Mediocrity of elected officials in a democracy;

3) Growth of a centralized bureaucratic state perfected in the France of Louis XIV and which Tocqueville felt was a danger as democracy in America grew;

4) Usurpation of the powers of the American States by the national government;

5) Weakening of public customs and manners of Americans that Tocqueville thought were the bedrock on which American laws were established; and

6) A passion for equality of condition that no laws can satisfy.

These were the great questions that American democracy faced in 1831 when Tocqueville visited America. Today we may add another question: Under pressure to reduce civil discourse to the lowest common denominator of "sound bytes," is it possible for American democracy to sustain public order and advance the common good without serious discussions? Indeed, what are the necessary conditions for a "healthy" democracy and can they be cultivated?

What did the Framers of the Constitution believe was possible when, in the Preamble to the Constitution of the United States, they declared that they sought *to form a more perfect Union, establish Justice, insure domestic Tranquility, provide for the common defence, promote the general Welfare, and secure the Blessings of Liberty to ourselves and our Posterity.* If it is possible to ask the question, "Can conscience be reconciled with the necessity of political order?" what has changed since that more optimistic year of 1787?

A phrase attributed to American Astronaut John Swigert, Jr., commander of the *Apollo 13* moon mission, burned these words into the consciousness of all Americans: "Houston, we have a problem." Today, "Houston" is America writ large. "We" have a problem.

"Regimes" have what Aristotle called "Constitutions" that provide the foundations of civic order. Democratic constitutions, especially, are unique because they are artificial, made, not naturally occurring, nor are they inherited from some ancient past. Nevertheless, democratic constitutions are not mere legal forms; they are interwoven with the character of their citizens. Shaping that character for self-government is essential for civic order. Unfortunately, we no longer do that.

The civil disturbances that roiled higher education in the late 1960s and early 1970s erased civic education from the required education of American college students. Political theorist Allan Bloom believed that was an important sign that "We," all of us, now have a very serious problem. Thus, we must ask again, whether American democracy itself is the source of our many problems or "We the People." Finally, we must ask, why do we give value to celebrities in areas outside the area of expertise that celebrated them? If an athlete excels in sport, for example, we give value to him beyond the range of skills in sport that made him famous.

Is the phenomenon of "Celebrity" endemic to democracy?

Is their presence, which we celebrate, due to a deficiency on our part that makes it difficult to discern greatness, character, and virtue in ordinary citizens?

Is a loss of our own virtue the root of this problem?

Are the technologies that now shape the modern era—high

speed computers, Internet browsers, broadcast and cable television, Facebook, Twitter, Instagram—reshaping America into a "Celebrity" culture or simply giving expression to celebrity in culture now shaped by digital communication?

Is the media,[2] or the messages conveyed by media, the problem and, if it is the messages, which messages?

Kim Kardashian, the many Rock, Punk and Rap musicians, Hollywood actors and actresses, television anchors, Televangelists and Talk Radio personalities that populate celebrity culture are influential, but is their influence consistent with civic order?

In recent memory, the State of Minnesota elected a former wrestler, Jesse Ventura, as its Governor, and a comedian, Al Franken, to the United States Senate. California elected a vaudeville dancer, George Murphy, and son of a heavy-weight boxing champion, John Tunney, to the United States Senate and a singer, Sonny Bono, to the U.S. House of Representatives. California also sent a former movie star, Ronald Reagan, to the Office of President of the United States, after electing him two times as Governor of California, an office to which Arnold Schwarzennegger was also elected. Yes, their names were all immediately recognizable when they stood for election, but "name recognition" does not convey value, "Celebrity" does. What does that tell us about our own non-celebrated lives?

Alexis de Tocqueville observed in *Democracy in America* that in the fifty years preceding 1831, the year he toured America, " ... the race of American statesmen has evidently dwindled most remarkably."[3] What happened between 1781 and 1831 gave Tocqueville the occasion to reflect upon the activity of the Continental Congress and the actions of Delegates to the Philadelphia Constitution, along with the range of presidents that followed George Washington,

---

[2] I'm using "media" as a singular noun.

[3] Alexis de Tocqueville, *Democracy in America*, Henry Reeve, trans. (CreateSpace Publishing, 2016). Chapter XIII: Government of the Democracy in America—Part I, p. 113.

from the election of President John Adams in 1796 to that of his son John Quincy Adams in 1824, followed by Andrew Jackson's election in 1828. Up to 1828, the United States enjoyed Presidents of great distinction.

George Washington	(1789-1797)
John Adams	(1797-1801)
Thomas Jefferson	(1801-1809)
James Madison	(1809-1817)
James Monroe	(1817-1825)
John Quincy Adams	(1825-1829)

And, then, Tocqueville observed, came mediocrity.

President Andrew Jackson had experienced deprivation and hunger as a child and imprisonment, slander, injuries in duels, and victory in battle as an adult, but d'Tocqueville saw little that recommended him for skill in, or knowledge, of government. Though Andrew Jackson served briefly in the U.S. House of Representatives and the U.S. Senate and was appointed to serve on the Tennessee Supreme Court, that service was incidental to his celebrity.

Andrew Jackson was a "celebrity" whose election in 1828 brought down the old order and introduced a form of popular democracy that was perfected by Progressives who in 1912 introduced the 17th Amendment to the Constitution of the United States. That amendment provided for direct election of members of the United States Senate and permanently reshaped American democratic government as we practice it today.

Andrew Jackson was followed by eight Presidents about whom the best we can say is that they came *before* America's great Civil War.

Martin van Buren	(1837-1841)
William Henry Harrison	(1841)
John Tyler	(1841-1845)

James Polk	(1845-1849)
Zachary Taylor	(1849-1850)
Millard Fillmore	(1850-1853)
Franklin Pierce	(1853-1857)
James Buchanan	(1857-1861)

Is it any different today? Upon whom in this list of one-term (if they were fortunate) ante-bellum Presidents may we assign "greatness"? Upon whom in this more contemporary list following the assassination of John F. Kennedy in 1963?

Lyndon B. Johnson	(1963-1969)
Richard Nixon	(1969-1974)
Gerald Ford	(1974-1977)
Jimmy Carter	(1977-1981)
Ronald Reagan	(1981-1989)
George H. W. Bush	(1989-1993)
Bill Clinton	(1993-2001)
George W. Bush	(2001-2009)
Barack Obama	(2009-2017)
Donald Trump	(2017-2021)
Joe Biden	(2021-)

If statesmanship is, and has been, dwindling or absent in American politics and the democracies of the West since 1828—close to two centuries as of this publication—then it is incumbent upon us to ask how long representative government may survive.

While American government was successfully shaped by the Philadelphia Convention of 1787 and ratification of the Constitution by the States that approved a "Bill of Rights," traditional political order in France was shredded by the French Revolution of 1789. It was this dissonance between those two experiences that brought Alexis de Tocqueville to America seeking to understand why democracy in America was successful. Let's return to that.

Tocqueville's *Democracy in America*

Alexis de Tocqueville understood that the damage done to France by Napoleon was made possible by French "men of letters." In France, intellectuals like Voltaire, Morelly, and the advocates of laissez-faire economics known as "Economists" lacked understanding of political freedom. That was not the case in America where, Tocqueville wrote, our leading men achieved a democratic revolution without having experienced "*The* Revolution." Tocqueville was right, the Americans had a revolution, but that revolution was not a killing field like the one that *esprit revolutionaire* inflicted upon 18th-century France.

By 1835 when Tocqueville published his study of American democracy, France had struggled for forty years to restore some semblance of stability, order, and justice of the *ancien régime* of France. Compared to the terrible inheritance of a destructive revolution that killed French nobles and ordinary citizens in the name of liberty and equality, Tocqueville counted the Americans blessed with achieving a democratic republic that offered freedom and equality to all without the murderous consequences that were inflicted upon France.

What was America's secret?

Maintenance of the American democratic republic, Tocqueville thought, was due to three factors:

1. the accidental situation in which Providence placed the Americans;
2. the laws; and
3. the manners and customs of the people.[4] (163)

---

[4] Alexis de Tocqueville, *Democracy in America*, Henry Reeve, trans. (CreateSpace Publishing, 2016). All citations placed in the body of the narrative are from the Henry Reeve, translation. This "Nook Book" is

Tocqueville takes up the subject of manners and customs, which Joseph Epstein remarks in *Alexis De Tocqueville: Democracy's Guide*[5] are central to his analysis, in chapter XVII of *Democracy in America*. Tocqueville entitled that chapter: "Principal Causes Maintaining The Democratic Republic."

When he was a young man, Tocqueville's reading of Voltaire and other *philosophes* caused him to suffer a loss of faith. Tocqueville battled that loss into his adult life and his emphases on religion, manners, and customs were part of his struggle to regain a religious certainty he once had. For Tocqueville, "customs, manners and opinions," bequeathed by the early settlers, "contribute most to the success of a republican form of government" (164). They were "the only durable and resisting power in a people" (161). Manners, by which he meant "habits, opinions, customs, and convictions" (181), are the moral and intellectual characteristics of social man (179).

A modern historian, David Hackett Fischer, much like Tocqueville, has analyzed the equivalent of what Tocqueville called "manners" in *Albion's Seed*.[6] There he outlines what Fischer calls enduring "Folkways" that shaped America:

- Geographic origin and reasons for colonizing
- Religion ways
- Order ways
- Liberty ways
- Food ways
- Language ways (accents)
- Magic ways

---

available online. Other translations are by Harvey C. Mansfield and Delba Winthrop (University of Chicago Press, 2002), Stephen D. Grant (Hackett Publishing, 2000), Gerald Bevan (Penguin, 13th printing, 2003) and Arthur Goldhammer (Library of America, 2004)

[5] Joseph Epstein, Alexis de Tocqueville, *Democracy's Guide* (New York, Harper Collins, Eminent Lives, 2006).

[6] David Hackett Fischer, *Albion's Seed* (Oxford, 1989).

- Marriage and courtship ways
- Child rearing ways

All these were aspects of the manners and customs of American culture that Tocqueville discovered simply by walking among the American people, talking to them about what they believed was important, and reflecting on that from his own experience. And lest we forget where these manners came from, Tocqueville made this observation:

"The organization and the establishment of democracy in Christendom is the great political problem of our time." (183)

Tocqueville believed that the attack on religion in the French Revolution challenged the stability, order, and morality of democracy in France and was an attack on Christian religion. In *The Old Régime and the French Revolution*, a book that has great meaning for Americans in our age of celebrity, he wrote, "By the 18th century Christianity had lost much of its hold on men's minds throughout Europe" and "in France, irreligion had become an all-prevailing passion..."[7] Today, in America and in Western Europe, few intellectuals are concerned that Western civilization has declined because few understand what Western Civilization is. Their attention and interests are captivated by a quest for understanding "Global Civilization."

Recovery of consciousness of the West was at the core of his exploration of democracy, for what, after all, did Tocqueville write *Democracy in America*, if it were not to recover ordered democracy in the West? In order to understand Tocqueville's argument we must appreciate his purpose. Tocqueville saw that "the influence of religious beliefs is shaken, the notion of divine right in decline, public morality vitiated, and that the notion of divine rights is declining; it

---

[7] Alexis de Tocqueville, *The Old Regime and the French Revolution*, trans. Stuart Gilbert (New York: Doubleday, 1983), 149.

is evident that public morality is vitiated, and the notion of moral rights is also disappearing" (140).

Also, Tocqueville was concerned that a passion for equality was awakened by democratic institutions that could never entirely satisfy that passion (115). He called that passion a "depraved taste" (37) and suggested that "if complete equality be our fate, is it not better to be leveled by free institutions than by despotic power?" (184). The pressure toward "complete equality" was "despotic." That *libido dominandi* is at the root of instability of democratic regimes. However, that was something from which the Americans were spared, at least, in 1831.

Tocqueville believed that the expanse of the American continent, given to Americans by a providential act of God, was the means for their remaining equal and free (164). With no enemies at their borders, the Americans could focus on peace, not war.

The laws were also important.

The early American colonies did not have to invent their laws, but inherited them from the English tradition of common law. And once arrived on a new continent, the American colonists exercised their independence by establishing laws suited to the new world. When, after the War of Independence, and a national government was required, they had the example of government in the former colonies and a clear sense of what kind of national government they wanted.

Where did this extraordinary ability of the Americans to fashion a government come from?

On this topic we find the core of Tocqueville's appreciation of Constitutional order. The Americans chose a "Federal" government and shaped the Constitution in a convention of delegates from the States, submitted it for Ratification, and amended it to include a Bill of Rights.

Here, too, he believed, Providence intervened.

Tocqueville said that one of the most fortunate incidents at the formation of the American Union was the accession of the Federalist Party because it gave the new republic time to acquire a certain stability. The "Federal" Constitution is a lasting monument to their patriotism and wisdom and was, in Tocqueville's mind, "the most perfect Federal constitution that ever existed" (98). In this appreciation for the Federalist Party, note the silent dismissal of Thomas Jefferson's Republican Democrats.

Tocqueville's organized cast of mind saw three circumstances contributing to the maintenance of a democratic republic:

1. a Federal form of government;
2. municipal institutions that limit despotism of the majority; and
3. the judicial power (168). Absent is commitment to natural rights.

But, the real strength of the country, he said, lies in the provincial, not the national government (85). Unlike France where, since Louis XIV, a complete, centralized government, had developed (55), the Constitution of the United States did not establish a centralized government. The Americans were too rooted in their independent and free municipalities (44). That was the regime that Tocqueville was anxious to visit in 1831.

Unlike native-born Americans, as a visitor to America, Tocqueville could say some things about America that were distasteful. There was, for example, the "singular paucity of distinguished political characters," which he attributed "to the ever-increasing activity of the despotism of the majority in the United States" (151).

Tocqueville found "... very few men who displayed any of that manly candor and that masculine independence of opinion which frequently distinguished the Americans in former times." (152). President Andrew Jackson, whom he met and described as "a man of violent temper and mediocre talents," was a prime example....no one circumstance in the whole course of his career ever proved that he is qualified to govern a free people, and indeed the majority of the enlightened classes of the Union has always been opposed to him (163).

Tocqueville believed that the American statesmen of 1831 "were very inferior to those who stood at the head of affairs" fifty years prior (115). There is so little distinguished talent among the heads of Government, he wrote, concluding that "the most able men in the United States are very rarely placed at the head of affairs" (115).

Of the American press, Tocqueville was even more dismissive. American journalists are poorly educated and of "a vulgar turn of mind" (108). Though Tocqueville had nothing but distain for journalists, he held the freedom of the press in high esteem. Liberty of the press is the only guarantee of liberty, he said (106), and he believed that it was good that no central control over expression of opinion exists in America (108).

His judgment was founded on the principle that where sovereignty of the people rules, "censorship of the press is not only dangerous, but it is absurd" (106), and in America the press is indispensable to the existence of freedom. That this freedom is incompatible with maintenance of public order is simply because liberty of the press requires that we submit to its inevitable evils (107). Only expansion of the numbers of journals of opinion can neutralize their bad effect (108).

Before a semblance of "objective" reporting occurred, the American press was used in the early days of the Republic to libel those with whom politicians disagreed politically. Truth was not the coin of the realm when it came to expression of opinions about the opposition. But libel is not as grievous as utilization of the press as it is today to impose a political religion.[8]

As a class, only lawyers met with Tocqueville's praise. After all, Tocqueville himself was a lawyer. What American lawyers learn in classes outside of precedents and principles of law tends to be ideo-

---

[8] See chapter 10, "Modern Political Religions" in my *The Development of Political Theory*. http://www.seewassim.com/book/browse.htm.

logically motivated and, as a class, lawyers today make up a powerful aspect of what Irving Kristol called the "new class—statist intellectuals, lawyers, social workers, educators et al."[9]

Tocqueville's *L'Ancien régime et la revolution*

So much of what Tocqueville writes in *L'Ancien régime et la revolution* seems familiar to contemporary American readers that we are compelled, if we love America as much as Tocqueville loved France, to study carefully what, in hindsight, Tocqueville believed was responsible for the destruction of the ancient order of society and politics of the great French nation.

Alexis de Tocqueville's study of democracy in America in 1831 was followed by his analysis of the revolution that beset the *ancien régime* of monarchical France. That analysis, published in 1856, is the best regime analysis since Aristotle organized the study of regimes into Constitutions. Every American concerned about great questions of political order today must study Tocqueville's little book. For, in that book may be discovered everything we need to know about political order, how it weakens and falls into decay, and lessons that may help us understand whether democracy in America today can be saved.

Tocqueville refers to key aspects of the history of France that led ineluctably to a centralized monarchy and violent reaction resulting in revolution as frustrations with an oppressive monarchy developed. Appreciation of what transpired in France is much like what Francis Graham Wilson described in his study of Spain. How can two monarchical regimes—of France and Spain—have any relevance for understanding democracy in America?

The first modern revolution experienced in France was shaped, not by foreign invaders, but by the actions of French monarchs—

---

[9] Jonah Goldberg, "Irving Kristol's Clear Thinking," *National Review*, September 23, 2009. https://www.nationalreview.com/2009/09/irving-kristols-clear-thinking-jonah-goldberg/

from the reign of Charles VII (1403-1461) to Louis XVI (1754-1793)—contributed to the growth of a centralized State. Here are their sins as recollected by Tocqueville:

a) Charles VII assumed the power to impose taxes without the consent of those who were taxed.

b) Louis XI (1423-1483) distributed titles of nobility in order to reduce the power of the nobility and withdrew the rights of municipalities.

c) Henry IV (1553-1610) lamented that nobles were leaving their lands thus leaving unattended their obligations to the peasants who remained. But, later in 17th century, it became common practice to lure the nobles to the Court.[10] French kings divided men "so as to better rule them."[11]

d) Louis XIV (1638-1715) granted and then reclaimed municipal rights of self-government in order to raise revenue. He engaged in the persecution of Huguenots at the same time that the language of "natural rights" of the *philosophes* became common.

e) Louis XVI foolishly considered the aristocracy a threat, not the urban masses congregated in the city of Paris.

Tocqueville cited key historical dates and events that in retrospect pointed to the outpouring of destructive violence that occurred in 1789.

Beginning in 1356, attitudes began to change sharply with the chaos caused by the captivity of King John at the battle of Poitiers. The insurrection of peasants in 1358 prefigured the periodic violence that erupted in France's history. That insurrection was called the "Jacquerie" because the nobility commonly referred to any peasant as Jacques, or Jacques Bonhomme. Another insurrection,

---

[10] Alexis de Tocqueville, *The Old Regime and the French Revolution*, trans. Stuart Gilbert (New York: Doubleday, 1983), 122.

[11] Ibid., 136.

which occurred in 1382 in response to the imposition of taxes, was called Mailotins because of iron mallots that the mob confiscated and used to attack business owners, government officials, and money lenders.

The year 1388 was marked by the madness of Charles VI (1368-1422) and the disorders of his rule that ensued. His reign was followed by the reign of King Charles VII who was permitted to impose a tax without the people's consent. Tocqueville writes, "...on that fateful day... the seeds were sown of almost all the vices and abuses which led to the violent downfall of the old régime."[12]

In 1591, a public uprising in Paris against the temporizing policies of Henry III is labeled the Council of the Sixteens. The head of the Catholic League led representatives of the sixteen *quartiers* of Paris arrested and executed three magistrates of the Parlement of Paris.

In 1648, the French nobility engaged in a last attempt in a series of wars, called the Fronde, to recover privileges usurped by French monarchs. Yet again, in 1685, Louis XIV disturbed civic order by arbitrarily placing dragoons in Protestant households as part of his persecution of the Huguenots.

The "War of Spanish Succession" (1701-1714) following the death of Charles II of Spain threatened the balance of power in Europe and led to war between the French and an alliance of England, the Dutch Republic, and Austria. Though the power of Louis XIV was challenged, the King secured the borders of France and continued his policy of centralization of state power.

In 1777, Maupeou, Chancellor of France, carrying out Louis XVI's reforms abolished the system of Parlements, or regional courts. Though the French had felt oppressed by the Parlements, with their abolition, Tocqueville writes, "had fallen the last barrier still capable of holding in check the monarch's absolute power."[13]

If there is one thing we learn from this historical narrative, it is

---

[12] Ibid., 99.
[13] Ibid., 166.

the danger to political order by centralization of the power of the State. Quite early in France, the local governments had been broken down and made way for a central administration staffed by a bureaucracy. Royal power was centralized in the *conseil du roi* or Royal Council.[14] Except for taxes negotiated directly by the Royal Council, "all other imposts such as the *taille*, which had in the past been entrusted to local officials capitation tax, and the *vingtièmes*, were assessed and levied directly by agents of the central government."[15]

A Controller General, had the whip hand,[16] and the Intendants—usually "a young man of humble extraction"—administered all local powers. That included conscription for military service, forced labor to repair roads and military barracks, the management of brigades of mounted police to enforce decisions of the Intendants, and selection of candidates for local office who were preferred by Intendants.

The assemblies in the parishes became an "empty show of freedom" with no power to put deliberations into effect.[17] French peasants bitterly resented "the idea of not having a say in the local administration of his village"[18] and, especially, the exemption of nobility and clergy from paying the *taille*. The nobles, stripped of any power, played no part in local government; remaining were "a horde of ignorant, uneducated peasants."[19]

"It would have been impossible to find," Tocqueville wrote, "in most parts of France, even ten men used to acting in concert and defending their interests without appealing to the central power for aid."[20]

France's men of letters exacerbated the desire to replace an odious system with something better. Their vision of a "perfect

---

[14] Ibid., 33.
[15] Ibid., 37.
[16] Ibid. 35.
[17] Ibid., 50.
[18] Ibid., 51.
[19] Ibid., 49.
[20] Ibid., 206.

State estranged the imagination of the masses from the here-and-now."[21] Voltaire, for example, envied the English for their freedom, but was indifferent to their political freedom. "He quite failed to realize that the former could not have survived for long without the latter."[22]

The revolution, which Tocqueville described as "a grim, terrific force of nature, a newfangled monster, red of tooth and claw"[23] was inevitably violent. "A nation so unused to acting for itself was bound to begin by wholesale destruction when it launched into a program of wholesale reform."[24] At the end, even the character of the French had been altered. The social habits created by despotic government included love of gain, fondness for business careers, a desire to get rich at all cost, a craving for material comfort. Easy living become "ruling passions."[25]

Beginning with the Presidential Administration of Woodrow Wilson, and exacerbated by the Great Depression, a vast, intrusive, centralized, bureaucratically administered State has taken control of government in the United States. That has an effect on American character as government service became plentiful.

Where before private careers in business or the professions were chosen, the stability and especially the benefits of government service became more attractive.

Where before, communities helped themselves recover from natural disasters, the first reaction of many Americans today is to look for support from the national government. Risks of hurricanes and earthquakes which can be avoided by not living on earthquake faults or on sea coasts were ignored in the belief that the government would make good what human folly created. In politics, how Presidents respond to natural disasters became tests for Presidents which could destroy their Administrations, if they failed.

---

[21] Ibid., 146.
[22] Ibid., 158.
[23] Ibid., 3.
[24] Ibid., 167.
[25] Ibid., xiii.

Moreover, an adversarial stance by American "Progressives" toward order, tradition, and religion has taken hold of our writers, artists, and even the poorest "educated" of our college graduates. Centralization of power and the adversarial culture of "Progressive" intellectuals assure that American political culture is in decline.

Members of Congress are held in such low public esteem that the times are ripe for non-politicians to make successful appeals for elective office though we are never quite sure what policies they will pursue. Lack of interest in political careers by our "best and bright-est" may be attributed to the New Class of "journalists" who be-lieve they are citizens of the world, and have no responsibilities a citizens of the United States.

Add to that an essential materialism that infuses American soci-ety and which Tocqueville associated with democratic regimes, and we may safely conclude that American political culture today is un-like other, more exuberant, eras that defined the American people.

After the French and Indian War, American colonists became conscious of shared interests independent from the British Crown. From that came the "Spirit of '76." Other positive eras were simi-larly defined: World War I (the Roaring Twenties) and World War II (anti-Communism) are two examples.

In 1991 the "Evil Empire" of the Soviet Union collapsed, thus releasing the energies of nations formerly subject to Russian totali-tarian control. But in the United States, American political leaders were defined by peripheral personal or ideological impulses, not central political virtues.

Jimmy Carter's impious moralism, George H. W. Bush's Kennebunkport "Internationalism," Bill Clinton's rapacious sexual appetite, George W. Bush's recovery from addiction and faith in democratic idealism and, of course, Donald J. Trump's "Celebrity" defined the Office of the President of the United States.

We would not be citizens of a democracy, if we didn't ask "What next?"

That question reveals some difficult problems. The ranks of

Congressional leaders are composed of the lackluster, the cunning, zealots, and utopian socialist politicians. None exist that gives confidence that after the next election we'll find anything better.

There is a long and term solution, however: change the culture. How can we do that?

1. First, in the short term, institute tough libel and slander laws and rebuke journalists who define themselves as "citizens of the world" and impose the ideology of "Globalism" on a public unaware of the ideological bias of the "news."

2. Second, over the long term, remove the Progressive Left from dominance in American higher education by starting new colleges and universities.

3. Third, begin a discussion about how to recover a commitment to civic education that prior to World War II was taught at every level of public education. That instruction in "Americanism" may not be a good fit for education in the United States today, but surely we should make American history and government and the history of Western civilization a central component of education in our high schools and colleges.

Do that, and Jesse Watters' "World" will feature interviews with sensible, knowledgeable citizens not unlike those who fought a war to establish the independence of the American colonies. But, what are the consequences, if we fail? Francis Graham Wilson examines those dark consequences.

Francis Graham Wilson's *Order and Legitimacy*

Half a century ago, Francis Graham Wilson published a study of Spanish traditionalist thought.[26] Wilson, a little known political

---

[26] Francis Graham Wilson, *Political Thought in National Spain: Order and Legitimacy*, Cheek, Power and Metallo, eds. Transaction Publishers. New

theorist teaching at the University of Illinois, was instrumental in focusing the attention of American conservatives to parallels between Spain and representative government in the United States. Are there any lessons for us Americans in this terrible history of Spain? It would seem not.

Rejection of the Protestant Reformation and the Enlightenment were critical to shaping traditionalist thought in Spain, and the Traditionalists took pride in Spain's influence at the Council of Trent and the truths affirmed in the Counter Reformation. Americans, on the other hand, rejected monarchical government in the War of Independence and had no national church but enshrined "freedom of religion" in these words of the First Amendment to the Constitution:

> Congress shall make no law respecting an establishment of religion, or prohibiting the free exercise thereof....

Add to that a dominant Protestantism of the American colonies through the early National period up through the American Civil War when Americans began to lose faith in Protestant Christianity.

What, then, is there to recommend in the Spanish traditionalist view of order? In asking that question, Wilson was ahead of his time. Like better known scholars, Eric Voegelin and Leo Strauss, Wilson was a student of classical philosophy and brought to his study an understanding of political order and the conflict between Enlightenment reasoning and traditional thought, but he was an American, unlike Strauss and Voegelin who were European émigrés. And he was a political conservative and a Catholic who appreciated the role of the Catholic Church in Spain and the animosity toward all religion of the French ideologues.

His study of Spanish political thought is an act of recovery of the writings and ideas of Spanish conservatives who, in their de-

---

Brunswick: 2004.

fense of tradition, political order and Christianity, were very much like American conservatives. Virtually unknown in America, few of the books and essays of Spanish traditionalists are available in English translations; thus, Graham and a few specialists kept their ideas alive for an English speaking audience.

American eyes and thoughts will turn to England or France, but Spain is more often an afterthought, a destination at the end of European vacation. Seldom is Spain an intellectual journey. Yet, disorders that are present in civil society in the United States in the 21st century were present in Spain in the 19th and 20th centuries. Spanish traditionalists who sought to avoid and overcome the failures of Spanish politics and culture, therefore, may be guides to understanding our own.

That is what Francis Graham Wilson thought.

In Roman times, the Iberian peninsula now occupied by Spain and Portugal was known as Hispania. In 711 AD, Hispania was invaded by the Umayyad Caliphate, one of four Caliphates formed after the death of Muhammad. Christian Europe was compelled to confront a rising Islam. Charles Martel pushed back Islamic raids into France in 732 AD, and in Hispania, now known as al-Andalus, Muslims were dominant for more than 780 years until the Reconquista in 1492 AD.

Ferdinand and Isabella ruled the Iberian peninsula and affirmed the Catholic faith as the official religion. Their grandson, Charles, established the Habsburg dynasty in Spain. Coinciding with the Habsburg dynasty, Spain experienced what is called a Golden Age in literature, art, and music. Calderon, Lope de Vega, Cervantes, Velazquez, composers of music such as Tomás Luis de Victoria, Francisco Guerrero, and others influenced Renaissance music.

In 1700, Charles II, the Spanish Habsburg ruler died and named the 16-year-old grandson of Louis XIV of France as his successor. Fearing a Spain controlled by France, a war of succession was waged by the Habsburgs whose Archduke Charles had support within Spain in league with France's rival England. Thus was waged a series of wars from 1702-1714 with major European rivals that left Spain weakened and divided. Ninety-four years later, Napoleon Bonaparte invaded the Iberian Peninsula.

Napoleon had led the military of revolutionary France in Egypt and Syria and returned to France in November 1799 where he was encouraged to overthrow the French government in a *coup d'etat*. The coup, known as the 18ᵗʰ Brumaire, *brume* being the second month of the Republican Calendar, became the rallying cry of revolutionaries through 1848.

In 1803, Napoleon, now First Consul of France, commenced a series of wars that by 1808 led to invasion of the Iberian Peninsula and the establishing of his brother, Joseph, as King of Spain. From 1808 through the Spanish Civil War (1936-1939), Spain was divided between those who resisted France's *esprit revolutionaire* and those who identified with a growing Liberal ideology.

Our difficulty in learning from the example of Spain's troubles may be traced to the dynastic character of Spain, the Catholic Church, and remaining misunderstandings with respect to the Spanish civil war of 1936-39. Moreover, the French Revolution that overthrew King Louis XVI of France and unleashed a revolution in ideas long before they were felt in America. Alexandra Wilhelmsen, historian of Spanish traditionalist thought, writes:

"...as far back as the Peninsular War, the more outspoken *realis-tas* had been countering liberal innovations with pleas for reform within the old order. In so doing, they had begun to develop a body of traditionalist thought that would culminate with Carlos VII and the writers who flocked to his cause in the late 1860s."[27]

With the introduction into Spain of *esprit revolutionaire* that accompanied Napoleon's conquest, many Spanish intellectuals turned

---

[27] Alexandra Wilhelmsen, "Carlos VII: An Introduction to Carlism," *Iberian Studies*, Vol. VIII (Spring, 1979), 29.

against the monarchy, the Catholic Church, and Spain's system of autonomous *fueros* founded (regions). Their influence led Fernando VII (1808-1833) to abrogate Spain's "Semi-Salic Law of Succession" that replaced his brother Carlos Maria Isidro (1788-1855) in line of succession to the Spanish throne in favor of the King's infant daughter, the future Isabel II. Fernando's wife, Maria Cristina (1806-1878), became regent and in effect ruled Spain until she herself was deposed.

Under her Minister, Juan Álvarez Mendizábal, the regime persecuted the Spanish Church, outlawed most male religious orders, shut down over 1,500 monasteries, closed the majority of schools and charitable institutions run by religious orders, abolished the tithe, and monitored religious publications.[28] The regime also confiscated Church property thus creating a new class that "owed its material well-being to the Revolution, thus increasing the number of supporters of the new liberal State."[29]

The King's brother, known as Carlos V to his supporters, was compelled to think through what was happening to his claim to the throne and, as consequence of his brother's actions, to Spain. Carlos V and Spanish traditionalists developed a political philosophy of traditionalism.[30] That doctrine became the principal opponent of *esprit revolutionaire* in Spain and the philosophy of "Carlism." Known as "The Pretender," in 1833 Carlos V led the first of four Carlist Wars, a split between members of the Royal Family that was mirrored in Spanish society.

During the life of Fernando VII, Spanish traditionalists, known

[28] Alexandra Wilhelmsen, "Antonio Aparisi y Guijarro: A Nineteenth Century Carlist Apologist for a Sacral Society in Spain," in James Lehrberger and M. E. Bradford, eds., *Saints, Sovereigns and Scholars* (Peter Lange, New York, 1993), 366.

[29] Ibid., 29.

[30] Alexandra Wilhelmsen, "The Theory of Spanish Political Traditionalism (1810-1875): Realism and Carlism," in *Identidad y Nacionalism en la Espana Contempranes: El Carlismo, 1833-1975*, Fundacion Hernando de Larramendi (Madrid, 1996).

as *realistas,* advocated:

1) acceptance "of the historical Catholic unity" of Spain;
2) advocacy of patria "or Fatherland"...in rejection of revolutionary ideas that were not Spanish;
3) rejection of a new Spain via liberal "constitutionalism." Spain was hundreds of years old, and that historical experience and institutional legacy was the basis of civil society;
4) advocated the Cortes, but with limited powers;
5) defense of regional autonomy or the *fueros*; a vigorous regional government and a small national government;
6) "sovereignty" represented in the person of the king, not by popular election; and
7) opposition to the Enlightenment notion of division of power, "the political realm should reflect...power...personified in the king."[31]

This program was summarized in four words, "God, Fatherland, Fueros, King."[32] After Carlos VII's death, the *realistas* became known as Carlists.

In 1967, in light of his reading in the history of traditionalism in Spain, Francis Graham Wilson was compelled to ask whether America would follow the course taken by Spain including acceptance of socialism, hostility toward limited government, and rejection of religion.

In searching for documents in which non-Spanish readers may find evidence of affirmation of traditional order in Spain, we can turn to Carlos V's "Manifesto to the Spaniards" of February 20, 1836,[33] and to the works of Donoso Cortés (1809-1853), Rev.

---

[31] Ibid., 48-51.

[32] Ibid., 51.

[33] Alexandra Wilhelmsen, "Political Theory of the Pretender Don Carlos," in *The Consortiium of Revolutionary Europe 1750-1850.* Proceedings, Athens, Georgia, 1985, 360.

Jaime Balmes (1810-1848), Marcelino Menéndez Pelayo (1856-1912), and Ramiro de Maeztu (1875-1936).

Perhaps best known, is Juan Donoso Cortés, a Spanish diplomat and descendant of the Spanish *Conquistador* Hernando Cortés (1485-1547), who destroyed the Aztec empire and brought Mexico under the sovereignty of the King of Castile. Like many Spanish intellectuals who came of age after the French Revolution, he was captivated by *esprit revolutionaire* until literally he was "mugged by reality" and realized that his earlier attraction to Jean-Jacques Rousseau and Rousseau's "General Will" was contrary to real political order. He countered that by affirming the universality of mankind and human solidarity. "…[H]umanity is a living and organic unity which absorbs all men, who in place of constituting it are only its instruments."[34]

Deeply religious, he wrote, "It is essential to [Liberalism] to repress alike all supreme affiliations and all radical negations, and thus, by means of discussion, it confounds all ideas and propagates skepticism."[35] And of "socialism" he wrote "The strength of socialism consists in its being a system of theology."[36] Donoso Cortés believe that the intellectual crisis of Europe was "too profound to be cured by liberal devices." Concession with the Enlightenment was impossible. Donoso turned to St. Augustine, Bossuet, and Vico.[37]

Rev. Jaime Balmes (1810-1848) would "second" Donoso Cortés' views: "the Catholic religion may fearlessly claim the gratitude of the human race, for she has civilized the nations who have professed her, and civilization is true liberty."[38] A Catholic priest, he opposed Luther who "sowed the seeds of endless trouble by the

---

[34] Ibid., 236.

[35] Ibid., 166.

[36] Ibid., 167.

[37] Francis Graham Wilson, *Political Thought in National Spain: Order and Legitimacy*, 28.

[38] Jaime Balmes, *European Civilization. Protestantism and Catholicity.* (Baltimore: John Murphy & Co., 1850), 281.

extravagant doctrine that a Christian is subject to no one." Rousseau he also rejected. "Rousseau is a miner who saps in order to overturn."[39]

In seeking a philosophy to counter Rousseau, Balmes turned to St. Thomas and his concept of just law which, derived from the eternal law, is binding on conscience. He wrote: "In that of St. Thomas, law is the expression of reason, in that of Rousseau, the expression of will; in the former, it is an application of the eternal law, in the latter, the product of general will."[40] We must remember the influence of St. Thomas among 19th-century Traditionalists when we later examine the closing of the soul of Catholic higher education in the United States.

Loss of that knowledge was lamented by Marcelino Menéndez Pelayo (1856-1912), a Spanish scholar who sought to recover the greatness of Spain's intellectual heritage. Best known for *Historia de las ideas estéticas en España* (1881–1891), his edition (1890–1903) of Lope de Vega, his *Antología de poetas líricos castellanos* (1890–1906), and his *Orígenes de la novela* (1905), Pelayo was nominated five times for a Nobel Prize in Literature.

In "Indications of Spain's Intellectual Activity in the Last Three Centuries," Menéndez Pelayo bemoaned that "[o]ur books are forgotten" and that "...intellectual activity in Spain was stifled during three centuries—the 16th, 17th and 18th."[41]

But, perhaps the most forceful advocate of Spanish Traditionalism was the political theorist, Ramiro de Maeztu (1875-1936), a member of the "Generation of '98" that faced the reality of Spain's decline after the Spanish-American War. He lamented the acceptance of "Humanism" that by the end of the 16th century had

---

[39] Ibid., 282.

[40] Ibid., 322.

[41] Papers prepared by Dr. H. Lee Cheek, Jr., for a Liberty Fund Conference, "Liberty and the Moral Life in the Works of Spanish Traditionalists and Francis Graham Wilson," January 22-25, 2009, Thomas Metallo, trans.

dominated Europe, which led to a loss of consciousness of man's living in sin.[42] That in turn shaped the idea of the "State" as supreme.

Maetzu traced the idea of the state from Hobbes who argued that the State was founded on necessity through Rousseau who asserted man's natural goodness and gave to the State "supreme, unique, and absolute power."[43] The unity of power of the state which all the political theories of the modern age affirm worked against the principle of subsidiarity. In Spain, stability had been given to political order by Corporate institutions, but the family, Church, and Guilds were dissolved by the discovery of human personality in the Renaissance. There were consequences: "the clergyman left the Church to become a humanist, a heretic, or the minister of a king."[44] The Landlords neglected their duties and saw in their properties only a source of income which they needed in order to live at Court.

In Germany, Maetzu argued, the state became an ethical ideal, and German children were taught that "goodness is immanent in the State."[45] Not only Germany, but "hedonistic ideology" in France came under Maetzu's critical eye as did laissez-faire economics.[46] Maetzu also lamented the lost opportunity to reshape Spanish university education. He felt that General Primo de Rivera was too busy "to engage in any popular education that might touch the people. The General had permitted all of the key positions in Spain, especially the professorships in the universities, to remain in the control of the liberal and socialist enemies of the Spanish tradition."[47] Maetzu's enemies were not too busy to forget him. He was

---

[42] Ramiro de Maeztu, *Authority, Liberty and Function in the Light of the War* (George Allen & Unwind, London, 1916), 16-7.

[43] Ibid., 21.

[44] Ibid., 24.

[45] Ibid., 38.

[46] Ibid., 114 and 186.

[47] Francis Graham Wilson, *Political Thought in National Spain: Order and Legitimacy*, 101.

executed in 1936 after the Nationalist uprising against the Second Republic.

Dynastic turmoil, which included the murder of Catholic priests and *esprit revolutionaire* that divided Spain, contributed to the departure of King Alfonso XIII, and the Second Republic was proclaimed in 1931. The brutal Spanish Civil War (1936-1939) found Leftists defending "the Republic" and traditionalists joining forces with the Spanish military to defeat a communist revolution. Francisco Franco defeated the revolutionaries and established an authoritarian regime that satisfied few except Franco sympathizers.

We begin to see some affinities with Spain after World War II when the recovery of Classical Philosophy by American scholars shaped the rejection of the influence of Rousseau. That rejection of the Enlightenment we shared with the Spanish traditionalists and some still affirm the natural law teaching of St. Thomas. The American defense of the Constitution as a fixed body of law founded on a philosophy of limited government is very similar also to the Traditionalist defense of traditional government.

Francis Graham Wilson emphasizes that we should not ignore "tradition" as an existing body of judgments or truth. Tradition "is a kind of deposit of political faith," he wrote, and a "profound attachment ... to a community of truth."[48] Integral to that community is a belief in Providence. Thus Donoso Cortes saw the hand of Providence when England was a balance to the power of Revolutionary France.[49]

Liberty, which we Americans cherish, originates in Christianity and religious truth. Many Americans affirm the truth of the Incarnation and the role of Christianity in shaping civilization in the West after the fall of the Roman Empire. Americans also share rejection of centralization of power in the administrative state. And American political conservatives share a love for the Liberal Arts and share

---

[48] Francis Graham Wilson, *Political Thought in National Spain: Order and Legitimacy*, 9.

[49] Ibid., 29.

the concern of Spanish traditionalists with the role of universities in shaping the intellectual classes.

Wilson writes, "The interpreters of a culture do not just happen. They are 'formed.' Is not this the most important of questions? Who makes the intellectuals—the writers, artists, and leaders of politics and religion—in a modern society?"[50]

Had the universities of Spain turned against revolutionary ideology, the tragic history of Spain's Civil War and the ultimate hold on the power of the state by an authoritarian military regime might have been avoided. That is an important lesson to remember as we come to appreciate the transformation of America's liberal university system into a Left University.

Are there signs in contemporary life that we may be heading down the road to discord and chaos from which Spain today has barely recovered?

Allan Bloom's *Closing of the American Mind*

In the late 1960s, revolutionary protests were directed at the conduct of the war in Vietnam and in advocacy of a "Civil Rights" movement. Leftist activists, assessing how best to capitalize on this unrest, concluded that revolution in the United States would not arise from America's working class and began to focus on American colleges and universities. When this occurred, the American system of higher education had changed and with increasing influence of the national government had become a "Left University."

As early as the Morrill Act of 1862, a system of Land Grant universities was founded that became a system of state universities.[51] And after the American Civil War, American colleges and universities began to break away from their religious moorings and higher education underwent a process of secularization. Then, the 1944 "GI Bill" flooded American colleges with returning GIs and,

---

[50] Ibid., 16.
[51] Today there are 76 "land grant" universities.

finally, the Higher Education Act of 1965 established a federal student loan program that has driven higher education finance to the present day. All Americans were given the opportunity to earn a college degree, but the large numbers of students entering college tested the limits of a system of higher education that had never accommodated enormous numbers of student enrollments.

By the mid-1960s, there was much to dissatisfy students especially at the large "mega universities" where they were crowded into large lecture halls and seldom met with faculty. Conditions were ripe for an explosion, and the University of California-Berkeley led an initial uprising against speech restrictions placed on student activists. The "Free Speech" movement at Berkeley elided into a national college-based movement against the war in Vietnam. Thus began a revolution in higher education perpetrated by student protestors.

Faced with rioting students, college administrators across the nation capitulated and granted student demands for removal of a core curricula of required courses and foreign language requirements. Procedures were established for review of faculty by students, and students were granted representation on college Boards of Trustees. The dummying-down of higher education in America had begun. In the late 1980s and early 1990s, calls for multicultural, gender, and African-American studies completed the decline of courses focused on Western civilization.

A former colleague of mine who taught at a major state university in Florida describes how the environment for scholarly discourse at his university changed over the period in time that Bloom examines in *The Closing of the American Mind*.

When I first joined the faculty, there was a core curriculum and there was a commitment to providing a liberal arts education. That is, there was recognition that there are skills and training (arts) needed by free (liberal) and responsible citizens in order to remain free. Faculty from different political views agreed that there was a tradition that had to be understood and there were thinking, reading, and writing skills that had to be acquired. Of course, that common purpose has completely disappeared. There is no effort to coordinate course offerings to provide any of the arts required to be free. There is also little or no intellectual engagement among the faculty.

When I first arrived, there was a sizable group from several fields and political perspectives that met regularly to discuss projects we were working on. These were not ideological harangues but serious intellectual engagement with topics of common interest— and the best criticism usually came from someone who was on the opposite side of the political aisle. Now, there are only clashes over ideological code words and other nonsense.

In 1968, Allan Bloom, then a professor of Government at Cornell University, was witness to these events as they occurred across the nation and specifically at Cornell University where complicit administrators and student radicals brought Cornell to its knees. The history of those "days of rage" at Cornell has been published by historian Dr. Tevi Troy in the Manhattan Institute's *City Journal*.[52] In an essay entitled "Cornell's Straight Flush," Troy recounts in detail what happened at Cornell. His account is a good way to come to terms with Allan Bloom's 1987 classic, *The Closing of the American Mind.*

Dr. Troy's story begins when James A. Perkins became the seventh President of Cornell University in 1963. Perkins had been chairman of the Board of the Negro College Fund and secured a quarter of a million dollar grant from the Rockefeller Foundation to increase the number of African-American students at Cornell. At the time, Cornell's enrollment was swelled by the post-World War II "baby boom" to 14,000 students.

Perkins actions increased the number of African-American students to 250. During the 1960s and 1970s, racial sensitivity was the hallmark of university professors and administrators. And the U.S.

---

[52] Tevi Troy, "Cornell's Straight Flush," *City Journal*, December 13, 2009.

government's "affirmative action" policies facilitated the college education of African-Americans. At Cornell, some black students felt alienated from the culture of white students and began take actions that thrust their feelings of alienation on the entire Cornell community.

In 1968 black students attempted to force the firing of a visiting professor of economics who had criticized economic development programs of some African countries. His class was disrupted. When he complained to the Chairman of his Department, his Chairman praised the disruptors for their activism. That established the principle that use of force for political ends at Cornell would not be punished, but would be approved by Liberal faculty and Cornell's administrators.

Black conservative economist and former U.S. Marine, Thomas Sowell, in his first academic position teaching economics at Cornell tried to eject a disruptive black student from his class, and was not supported by his Chairman. Sowell saw the writing on the wall and resigned his academic position. Thirty years later, Sowell wrote in *The Weekly Standard* that that these students were "hoodlums" with "serious academic problems [and] admitted under lower academic standards," and he noted "it so happens that the pervasive racism that black students supposedly encountered at every turn on campus and in town was not apparent to me during the four years that I taught at Cornell and lived in Ithaca."[53]

At a Symposium on South Africa in 1969, President Perkins was physically assaulted by a black sophomore student. Perkins fled the auditorium. In April of that year, black students took control of Willard Straight Hall, Cornell's student activity center. Visiting parents of Cornell students who were staying in Straight while visiting their children were driven outside by disruptive black students. When these parents appealed to campus security officials, they were told that campus police could do nothing.

---

[53]   Thomas   Sowell,   *The   Day   Cornell   Died*,   https://www. hoover.org/research/day-cornell-died

Student radicals chained the entrances to Straight and brought rifles into the building. Armed black students demanded nullification of actions against disruptive students from the previous year, commencement of negotiations concerning housing for black students, and investigation of a cross burning on campus which campus police believed was started by black activists. Negotiations ensued, black students left Straight, but no students, including those wielding rifles, were punished.

Allan Bloom was shocked by these and subsequent actions by spineless Cornell administrators and, like Thomas Sowell, left Cornell. Eighteen years later, Bloom published *The Closing of the American Mind*. About these events, Bloom wrote:

> I know of nothing positive coming from that period, it was an unmitigated disaster for them. I hear that the good things were "greater openness," "less rigidity," "freedom from authority," etc.—but these have no content and express no view of what is wanted from a university education.[54]

I, too, share Allan Bloom's judgment of the demands of student rioters of the 1960's. In the Fall, Michaelmas term, in 1968, I was at the London School of Economics when students shut down the LSE and barged into Michael Oakeshott's classroom and threatened him and us with injury if we did not leave. Many of those disruptive students were undergraduates who had been expelled from Columbia University for rioting during the Spring of 1968, but were admitted to continue their studies at the London School of Economics.

The Left University was taking care of its own.

The Closing of the American Mind should be seen, therefore, as a commentary on American higher education at a time when it was

---

[54] Allan Bloom, *The Closing of the American Mind* (Simon and Schuster: New York, 1987), 320. All pages from *Closing of the American Mind* are cited in the body of the text.

torn from its moorings in the tradition of liberal education and became ideological by focusing on globalism, multiculturalism, and identity studies.

One such "movement" is the recognition of "Women's Studies" as an academic discipline. Women's liberation, the sexual revolution, and an underlying feminist ideology became powerful forces in American higher education. Feminism, Bloom argued, sought "a liberation from nature" more than a liberation from convention (99). Since nature is fixed, the aspiration to be liberated from nature requires the fashioning of a substitute, pseudo reality rooted in will. Bloom describes this as "the longing for the unlimited, the unconstrained" (100). What are the consequences of such longing?

> It ends as do many modern movements that seek abstract justice, in forgetting nature and using force to refashion human beings to secure that justice. (100)

In other words, the feminist movement is willing to use force against those who oppose it. That "force" can take the form of charges of sexual harassment. Today, the "Feminist movement" has contributed to university and work environments tense with concern by men that charges of sexual harassment can be used to destroy the professional careers of male colleagues. Bloom suggests that university feminists will force men to conform to their interests—or else.

Allen Bloom's *Closing of the American Mind*[55] must be seen in the context of a transformation of the traditional liberal university formalized in the 19th century into what James Piereson calls a "Left University" in the 20th century. That transformation was realized during the years 1968 to 1987.

A child prodigy, Bloom enrolled in the University of Chicago's

---

[55] All citations are from Allan Bloom, *The Closing of the American Mind: How Higher Education Has Failed Democracy and Impoverished the Soul's of Today's Students* (New York: Simon and Shuster, 1987).

humanities program for gifted students at age fifteen and graduated at age eighteen when most American students enter college. As an undergraduate his tutor was the classicist David Grene, and, as a graduate student at the University of Chicago, he encountered the philosopher, Leo Strauss.

Bloom thus was educated as a classicist in what political theorists refer to as the Straussian "school" of political theory. That Straussian approach required that Bloom hone skills in analysis rooted in deep study of classical political philosophy, but also the political theory of "the Moderns."[56] As such, Bloom may be considered a "modern," and though few modern scholars survive Bloom's criticism including Max Weber, John Rawls, Robert Dahl, Claude Lévi-Strauss, Carl Becker, and David Riesman, Bloom stood firmly in the camp of Enlightenment philosophy.

Thus, underlying Bloom's analysis of intellectual forces that literally close the minds to truth can be found a "divided self," enamored of Socrates, Plato and Aristotle, but also appreciative of the reasoning of John Locke, Jean-Jacques Rousseau, and Friedrich Nietzsche. From Socrates, Plato, and Aristotle, Bloom learned that there is objective truth which can be known and that a failure to teach that truth "is" has had a deleterious and destructive influence on civic order. Relativism and a growing nihilism that afflict intellectual culture in America is the result of this "value relativism." Bloom believed that relativism contributed to the fragility of families and incidences of divorce.

We can see from a close reading of *The Closing of the American Mind* that Bloom clearly loved the experience growing up in Chicago with his family and was dismayed that so many of his students were adversely affected by the divorce of their parents. Bloom believed that the American family was in decline because the individualism that is part and parcel of democracy works to exacerbate the self-interest of individuals. The family, however, entails attachments

---

[56] See Richard Bishirjian, "Leo Strauss and the American Political Religion," *Modern Age* (Fall 2014), 7-18.

to others and thus establishes relationships that resist the isolation of individuals.

Parents, husbands, wives, and children are hostages to the community. They palliate indifference to it and provide a material stake in the future. This is not quite instinctive love of country, but it is love of country for love of one's own. It is the gentle form of patriotism, one that flows most easily out of self-interest, without the demand for much self-denial. The decay of the family means that community would require extreme self-abnegation in an era when there is no good reason for anything but self-indulgence (86).

Add to American individualism the mobility provided by modern transportation that can facilitate employment far away from family and school friends. That is not the case in Canada or France, Bloom observes, where mobility is more restricted. Consequently, Americans invest less in their past and the people from their past than citizens of other countries. The effect of this is to shape the souls of Americans by making them "spiritually unclad, unconnected, isolated, with no inherited or conditional connection with anything or anyone" (89). Bloom likens this to Plato's description of democratic youths,[57] dedicated to equality, preoccupied with themselves, and treating all things equally because there is no right, no wrong, nothing absolutely true, no life better than another. (88)

Bloom denigrates our popular notion of "lifestyles," the defense of which has become a moral cause. "In America," Bloom observes, "there is always a need for moral justification." (234) And lifestyles can be justified because lifestyle involves no reasoning and does not require any form of intellectual or artistic achievement. "Life-style is so much freer, easier, more authentic and democratic. No attention has to be paid to content" (235). Whatever you choose is good.

Here, Bloom sees the relevance of Tocqueville who understood that in a democracy abstractions have the power to change every-

---

[57] *Republic*, 561c-d.

thing (235). This susceptibility to change and moral relativism works itself out in divorces. It is very unusual for a political theorist to address issues like divorce, but Bloom was disturbed by the effects of divorce on his students. Writing in the late 1980s, Bloom called divorce "America's most urgent social problem" (119).[58]

That is true, he believed, on several levels.

Children subjected to divorce view the world in terms of conditional relationships. A capriciousness enters their lives that challenges what should not be challenged—the "unbreakable bond, for better or for worse, between human beings" (119). And the fatuous concerns of students for "self-determination, respect for other people's rights and decisions, the need to work out one's individual values and commitments" hide what Bloom calls "a thin veneer over boundless seas of rage, doubt and fear" (120). Compared to European students, Bloom writes, Americans seem like barbarians.

The schools of Europe are simply better, but European students are raised in a homogenous racial and ethnic culture quite unlike America. The United States has good preparatory schools where the wealthy send their children, but these are the children of elites whose family traditions include education at places like Harvard, Princeton and Yale.

Normal, "ordinary" Americans may come from prosperous families of professionals or business owners, but somehow they don't look, sound, of think of themselves as elite. For Bloom, that is what he calls their "charm." They exhibit natural curiosity and experience love of knowledge that came to them "in the first flush of maturity" (48). Learning for them was not "old hat," but vital and living in them with serious consequences for the remainder of their lives.

---

[58] "...researchers have found that the rate of divorce in the U.S. actually peaked at about 40% around 1980 and has been declining ever since. And, according to data from the National Survey of Family Growth, the probability of a first marriage lasting at least a decade was 68% for women and 70% for men between 2006 and 2010. The probability that they would make it 20 years was 52% for women and 56% for men.

Without traditional constraints or encouragements, without society's rewards and punishments, without snobbism or exclusivity, some Americans discovered that they had a boundless thirst for significant awareness, that their souls had spaces of which they were unaware and which cried out for furnishing (48). These are the exceptions and many—too many—students are then, and are now, addicted to rock music. On this topic, Bloom is adamant. "This is the age of music and the states of soul that accompany it."

Rock music is king and very few students have any familiarity with classical music (69). Rock music responds to students' sexual desire. They understand that "rock has the beat of sexual intercourse." Feeding that desire is a music industry whose market is children. The rock business is perfect capitalism, supplying to demand the frequently-cited "half."[59] It has all the moral dignity of drug trafficking, but it was so totally new and unexpected that nobody thought to control it, and now it is too late (76).

Bloom reminds us that Plato took music seriously (70) and believes that we should, too. In Plato's *Republic*, the discussants seeking to know what is the best regime agree that music should be taught first, even before gymnastics (376e). Censorship is an aspect of the best city developed in Plato's *Republic*, and music is not exempted. Music that is permitted will exclude "wailing and lamentations" (398e),[60] but harmonic modes are allowed. Only the rhythms of an orderly and courageous life are permitted (399e). Appendix B tracks Billboard's Best Singles from 1942 to 2016. Very few of these "best" singles would be acceptable in Plato's best regime.

Though Bloom was deeply rooted in ancient Greek philosophy, he was intimately familiar with the Enlightenment which he describes as "the first philosophically inspired 'movement,' a theoreti-

---

[59] Sarah Jacoby, "What the divorce rate really means," online at "refinery29." http://www.refinery29.com/2017/01/137440/divorce-rate-in-america-statistics

[60] Plato, *The Republic of Plato*, Allan Bloom, trans. (New York: Basic Books, 1968), 77.

cal school that is a political force at the same time" (262). Bloom
lists these Enlightenment thinkers as "men like Machiavelli Bacon,
Montaigne, Hobbes, Descartes, Spinoza and Locke, along with the
eighteenth-century thinkers like Montesquieu, Diderot and Voltaire." Bloom does not castigate them as revolutionary in the negative sense used by non-Straussian theorists including Tocqueville
who collectively defined them as advocates of *esprit revolutionaire*.
This is an anomaly in *The Closing of the American Mind* and in the
Straussian "School" that accepted the Enlightenment as having replaced the classical and medieval traditions of political theory.[61]

Bloom finds good in the Enlightenment even as he rails against
the forces, attributable to the Enlighentment, that contribute to
decline of civic culture. Take, for example, what Bloom has to say
about "values." Values, Bloom writes, are a "new language of good
and evil" designed to prevent us "from talking with any conviction
about good and evil" (141). Values are based in will and thus they
cannot be "discovered by reason, and it is fruitless to seek them to
find the truth or the good life (143).

A society in which its citizens believe that truth is relative, or
with significant numbers of citizens who deny that truth can be
known and taught, will be susceptible to greater forces that use
power to achieve their own goals. For that reason, Bloom writes
with what can only be called frustration that "[t]here is one thing a
professor can be absolutely certain of: almost every student entering the university believes, or says he believes, that truth is relative"
(25). Students come to this view because they believe that a free society must be tolerant. "Relativism is necessary to openness; and
this is the virtue" (26). American universities are accomplices in this
failure of insight because they see education as the means to
providing students with the moral virtue of "openness." Where before we educated citizens to be Americans, we now seek to create
the "democratic personality." Bloom calls this the replacement of

---

[61] Richard Bishirjian, "Leo Strauss and the American Political Religion," *Modern Age* (Fall 2014), 7-18.

the natural soul with an artificial one (30).

Clearly, Bloom sees the university in a democracy as a source of disorder. At Cornell, administrators sought to do good by providing an education to minorities who misused that opportunity to engage in destructive practices. President Perkins established permanent racial quotas in admissions, gave preference to racial minorities in financial assistance, engaged in racially motivated hiring of faculty, and made it difficult for faculty to give failing marks (95).

Irving Babbitt and John Erskine, were loudly critical of these "reforms" in higher education that removed the "Core Curricula" of required courses. Erskine introduced a core honors curriculum at Columbia University in the masterpieces of Western philosophy. That core curriculum remains today at Columbia and another at the University of Chicago founded by Mortimer Adler and Robert Hutchins. Liberal Arts colleges with core Great Books curricula are the remnants of what was once a vibrant tradition of classical education. That is unfortunate because the Great Books compel scholars to remember the past and to retrieve important lessons learned by the most important minds of Western civilization.

Replacing core curricula with gender, African-American or "global" studies ignores where we came from, who we are and how we should act as citizens of the West. When that basis is removed from higher education, the virus of moral relativism cannot be confronted by scholarship leading to discovery of truth because only "opinion" has value. If there is no "Truth" that can be discovered, what is left for us to search for but self-interest. If there is no "Common Good," then to what can we appeal in the face of the demands of the powerful? If the appetites of the young are aroused by Rock, Rap, and other musical trends, how can we instruct them about virtue? If a democratic regime values equality of condition, what will become of the equal protection of the law or any of the limits placed on the power of the state by a philosophy of limited government enshrined in the Constitution of the United States?

6.

The Left University

Alexis de Tocqueville was aware that revolutionary ideas destroyed the *ancien régime* in France and, as we've seen, those ideas were carried to America in the many political religions that have disrupted American politics. Perhaps Americans were more susceptible to the influence of *esprit revolutionaire* because, he observed, "[w]hen once Americans have taken up an idea, whether it be well or ill founded, nothing is more difficult than eradicating it from the their minds."[1]

Spain was another example. From 1808 through the Spanish Civil War (1936-1939), Spain was divided between those who resisted France's *esprit revolutionaire* and those who identified with a growing Liberal ideology. Revolutionary ideas appeal to academics, and Spanish political theorist Ramiro de Maeztu (1875-1936) lamented that General Primo de Rivera, Prime Minister of Spain from 1923 to 1930, was too busy "to engage in any popular education that might touch the people. The General had permitted all of the key positions in Spain, especially the professorships in the universities, to remain in the control of the liberal and socialist enemies of the Spanish tradition."[2] Maeztu felt that Spanish universities were, in part, responsible for civil disorder.

Allan Bloom also believed that universities are a primary force infecting civil society with notions about "values," "lifestyles," and other evidence of value relativism. Where before we educated citizens to be Americans, Bloom wrote, we now seek to create the "democratic personality." Bloom calls this the replacement of the

---

[1] *Democracy in America*, 109.

[2] Francis Graham Wilson, *Political Thought in National Spain: Order and Legitimacy*, 101.

natural soul with an artificial one.[3] If fragility of social order is the result of "artificial" souls, James Piereson believes, that may be attributed to a transformation that occurred when a dominant "liberal" university system in America was transformed into a "Left University" and was integrated into a system of economic management largely constructed by the British economist, John Maynard Keynes.

Piereson, one of the best chroniclers of the destructive role that the American university system plays in American society, is well-equipped for this role by his university teaching (Iowa State, Indiana University and the University of Pennsylvania), grant management, first with the Olin Foundation and now the William E. Simon Foundation, and prolific writing on subjects dealing with education. Perhaps his best statement on the problem of higher education in the United States was published under the title, "The Left University," in the *Weekly Standard* in 2005. We examine it here in an updated version of a chapter by the same title in *Shattered Consensus*, published in 2015 by Encounter Books.

Piereson asks if and when we may expect another revolution that puts civil society on better ground. For Piereson that revolution, equivalent to the New Deal, will necessarily counter the ideas of John Maynard Keynes. Placing this in context, Piereson observes that the United States has experienced three revolutions; Thomas Jefferson's victory over the Federalists (1800), the Civil War (1865) and the New Deal (1935). Each represented a "regime."

The first regime promoted democracy, the second industrialization, and the third, economic security. Piereson believes that a "fourth regime" is possible that overturns the welfare state and initiates a new phase of growth and dynamism[4] (82-83). This will oc-

---

[3] Allan Bloom, *The Closing of the American Mind*, 30.

[4] James Piereson, *Shattered Consensus: The Rise and Decline of America's Postwar Political Order* (Encounter Books, New York, 2015). All citations are cited in the text.

cur when a party or candidate arises that bypasses the interest group system of rent-seeking coalitions. Let's examine how Piereson came to this conclusion.

Shattered Consensus begins with an examination of Keynes idea of the managed state, a revolutionary perspective that quickly dominated economic thought when first propounded in two books: *The Economic Consequences of the Peace* (1919) and *General Theory of Employment, Interest and Money* (1936). Keynes was one of three giants of economic thought, what some call the "political philosophers" of the 20th century: Keynes, Hayek, and Schumpeter (20-21). Of the three, "...Keynes exercised by far the greatest influence in the post-Depression and postwar era. More than Hayek, Schumpeter, or any other economist of the time, Keynes went beyond diagnosis to offer practical remedies for the economic crisis of the 1930s" (21).

Ironically, Keynes's "enterprise," as Piereson calls it, is vulnerable "not primarily because the economic theory is flawed, but because it cannot be made to work from a political point of view" (19-20). For that reason, Piereson believes not merely that removing Keynes' influence from the fabric of national politics is critical, but removal of his influence can be accomplished.

What was Keynes's "enterprise"?

Keynes envisioned an emerging system of capitalism in which large business enterprises and not-for-profit institutions operated alongside government in common efforts to promote the public interest. The friction between the public and private spheres, so much an aspect of the old order of liberalism, was giving way to a new order of cooperation among large institutions. Keynes's corpororatist vision of the capitalist order represented an evolution of liberalism beyond its nineteenth-century emphasis on individuals, competition, and suspicion of the state (23).

As we saw, Tocqueville was aware that centralization of power—developed to a fine art in France from Charles VII to Louis XIVI—carried enormous dangers for democratic regimes. Francis

Graham Wilson's examination of Spanish "Traditionalism" considered centralization of power dangerous to the principles that supported democracy in Spain. Yet, despite the overwhelming historical judgment that centralization must be constrained, John Maynard Keynes's political economy was based on the assumption that limits on government supported by the 19th-century free market theories of classical liberalism were simply inadequate to modern conditions.

In order to address that weakness, Keynes was an advocate for empowering national government with "new managerial duties" to supplant free exchange of goods and limited state power with "a system of capitalism in which large business, not for profits and the government operated to promote the public interest" (22-23). Diminished in influence, if not superseded by the state, were the unfettered actions of "banks, the wealthy and investment houses."

Piereson observes that to accomplish this, Keynes rejected "three postulates of classical economics."

1) Says Law, which holds that supply creates demand;
2) Rejection of widespread unemployment as a consequence of business cycles;
3) Rejection of the practice of "saving," which Keynes considered to be "leakage" from demand (30) or withdrawal of consumption.(31)

Prosperity lay in consumption and debt, not thrift and saving. Those assumptions were present in a second stage of New Deal programs of President Franklin D. Roosevelt, called the "Second New Deal," that made significant changes in the administration and purpose of the American economy.

The Social Security Act created an "entitlement" that, accompanied by new entitlements introduced by FDR's successors— Medicare, Medicaid, subsidized lending for college tuition, and prescription medicine benefits—placed permanent economic burdens on the American taxpayer and created coalitions of "rent seekers." (48). Added to Social Security, in FDR's "Second New Deal," were the National Labor Relations Act that established a basis for union power, and the Revenue Act of 1935, which raised the marginal tax rate to 78%. Despite those "reforms," Piereson observes, unemployment never fell below 14% during FDR's second term (56).

Federal spending was 2.5% of GDP at the onset of the Great Depression, increased to 10% of GDP by 1940 "on the eve of World War II, then increased four or fivefold during the war years before stabilizing throughout the postwar era at around 20% of GDP—or at a level large enough to finance Keynesian style policies" (42-43). To use a common phrase of the time, America was "cooking with gas."

Despite this history of failure, Piereson observes that liberals and progressives over the past five decades have called for yet another "New Deal." The most recent, Thomas Piketty, an economist at the Paris School of Economics, has made a case against "inequality" that de-emphasizes traditional concerns—in America, at least—for freedom, innovation, and growth. Piketty's solution: increase marginal tax rates to 80% on the very rich and 60% on incomes between $200,000 and $500,000 (71).

Significantly, Piketty, is an "academic."

Home to academics in America is a Left University system, a system that is the result of having been taken over by liberals and radicals. One statistic indicating that something strange has occurred may be seen in estimates of faculty, identified as conservative, who teach in the Humanities and Social Sciences. That number is so low that Piereson calls the American university equivalent to a "one- party state" (264) and a system characteristic of universities in "banana republics" (266).

Just as the faculty on American colleges and universities has moved to the Left, so the purpose of education has been altered.

Through the colonial period, Piereson writes, the purpose of colleges was "to shape character and to transmit knowledge and right principles to the young in order to prepare them for vocations in teaching, the ministry, and the law" (266). There weren't many colleges nor skilled philosophers, but the few there were had an influence in educating the generation that won the War of Independence and framed the Constitution.

At the College of New Jersey that became Princeton, John Witherspoon instructed James Madison in the ancient philosophy of Plato and Aristotle. At William and Mary in Virginia, William Small, a scientist and medical doctor, instructed Thomas Jefferson in the works of John Locke, Adam Smith, and David Hume. Jefferson later wrote, "from his conversation I got my first views of the expansion of science and of the system of things in which we are placed."[5]

The system of education in the early national period of American government was transformed over time and Piereson plots the course of that development. Between the years 1870 and 1910, a modern academic enterprise took shape. Under the influence of German education exemplified by Wilhelm von Humbolt, founder of Humbolt University in Berlin, graduate education and electives developed during this time. New universities were established: Chicago, Johns Hopkins, Stanford, and Vanderbilt led by visionary university presidents, Charles Eliot (Harvard), Daniel Coit Gilman (Johns Hopkins), Andrew White (Cornell), William Rainey Harper (Chicago), David Starr Jordan (Stanford) and Woodrow Wilson (Princeton).

The modern university moved away from looking to ancient writers for moral lessons and political guidance. Piereson attributes this to German Idealism's belief that "truth is not something known and passed on, but the product of persistent inquiry and

---

[5] Ganter, Herbert L. "William Small, Jefferson's Beloved Teacher," *William and Mary Quarterly*, 3rd Ser., Vol. 4, No. 4 (Oct., 1947), 505–11.

continuous revision" (371). As we saw in Chapter 3, German ideal-ism was an important aspect of the creation of "political religions" that defaced the West in totalitarian movements of the 20th centu-ry.

While a secular, political, religion was germinating, American faculty members were placed at the center of the academic enter-prise and empowered to decide all matters dealing with curriculum, tenure, and hiring. Thus emerged what Piereson calls "a new class of professional intellectuals" (370- 373).

The totalitarian temptation in political religion in America was deterred by more practical pursuits that interested this "new class" of professional intellectuals. Progressives leapt into action and fash-ioned the first phase of modem liberalism with a focus on making academics handmaidens of government. Leaders in this develop-ment were critics of Scottish "common sense" philosophers of the Scottish Enlightenment and British empiricism.[6]

Gone were David Hume, Adam Smith, Thomas Reid, Adam Ferguson, James Beattie, and Dugald Stewart. In their place stepped Thorstein Veblen (economics), John Dewey (philosophy), Charles Beard (history), and Oliver Wendell Holmes (law). Piereson ob-serves that "these thinkers were not only academics but more im-portantly graduates of the new university. All believed that the Constitution was "inadequate to the challenge of modern life" (274). Thus followed reorientation from an order defined by classi-cal liberalism and appreciation of freedom to government power used for the public interest and supported by academic "experts."

In the late 1890s, the University of Wisconsin formalized what came to be known as the "Wisconsin idea" by which universities partnered with the state to provide technical expertise to guide state legislators (275). The Wisconsin idea brought out into the open a new role for the university, which was to bring experts and expert

---

[6] See "Scottish Philosophy in the 18th Century" the Stanford Ency-clopedia of Philosophy online at plato.stanford.edu/entries/scottish-18th.

knowledge into the political process. This was one of the clearest links between the emerging university and the Progressive movement since the university was the logical source for the experts needed to design and implement Progressive policies (275).

The Left University came into existence as other changes in higher education were occurring. Single-sex colleges disappeared, the regulation of student morals disappeared, government regulation of employment expanded, and pressure was placed on institutions to hire women and minorities. The lines between teaching and advocating political positions became blurred, and campus radicals asserted that all teaching was "political."

Core curricular requirements were eliminated and political correctness (PC) came to replace the liberal underpinnings of teaching and research. New types of professors to teach PC subjects (Ward Churchill, Native American Studies at CU-Boulder) and a variety of race hustlers were hired to teach African-American Studies (Cornell West at Princeton). A doctrine of group representation of women, minorities, identity politics, and diversity studies took hold (279-282).

Throughout American higher education, an official civil religion consisting of the utopian dream of absolute equality is indoctrinated in African-American students that engenders disaffection from the history of their country and the bludgeoning of white students to accept white guilt. Other ideological propaganda is foisted on women students in "Women's Studies."

At Colorado University-Boulder, the Department of Women and Gender Studies "educates" one hundred Department Majors in "how gender affects social movements and politics, the histories of sexuality and gender politics in Latin America, feminist political philosophy, global justice, violence against women, and feminist literature and cinema."[7]

At the University of Southern California, a "Diversity Summit"

---

[7] https://www.colorado.edu/wgst/

was convened in one Department. Conducted over four days "devoted to dialogue around issues of race, gender, culture and identity —not only in our School, but throughout our field."[8] USC's President, C.L. Max Nikias, educated as an electrical engineer,[9] has dedicated USC to maximization of diversity throughout the university.[10] Continuing the departure from understanding our citizenship in Western civilization, President Nikias argues in his annual presidential address that "It is by embracing every culture ... every religious view, every individual, that we find ourselves."

For those not trained as engineers, careers in academe and government are made by publishing books on topics favored by the Left University and by earning graduate degrees at "the best" institutions such as Harvard, Yale, Princeton, CU-Boulder, and USC. A typical case is former Ambassador to the United Nations, Samantha Powers, an ideologically motivated Leftist with a "Johnny one-note" interest in "global justice" and the pursuit of power. Her ability to discern common interests with the wealthy and powerful led her to Gregory Carr and the staff of a junior Senator from Illinois, Barack Obama. Powers parlayed that position into work on the Obama Presidential campaign and appointment as U.N. Ambassador.

Powers' career indicates what the "fast track" to success within the Left University system requires, namely as follows:

1) a major prize for publishing in an area of Left University interest;

2) a patron who is, essentially, uneducated, but extremely wealthy;

---

[8] https://dramaticarts.usc.edu/evoking-change/

[9] Engineers are popular choices for university president because they are ignorant of philosophy, literature, culture, theology, American history, and Constitutional Law.

[10] http://news.usc.edu/91693/nikias-puts-spotlight-on-diversity-in-annual-presidential-address/

3) a Harvard law degree; and

4) affiliation with the Kennedy School at Harvard University which attracts endowments for ideological area studies from wealthy benefactors.[11]

Piereson concludes that just as British power declined as British universities were politicized, so a parallel may be seen in the growth of the Left University in the United States.

---

[11] Formerly located at https://dickbishirjian.com/2017/09/21/path-to-success-for-leftists

7.

Closing of the American Soul to Religion

In the year 2000, I founded a for-profit Internet university and recruited scholars rooted in traditional scholarship to join a venture that I described as "Conservative."

From the invasion of Europe by Napoleon and the forming of a "Progressive" movement in late 19th century, universities in Europe and the United States had become dominated by anti-traditional ideologies. I thought that my new venture would attract allies at the many religious colleges in American higher education, but I found that many Protestant and Catholic colleges and universities were no longer committed to the faith of their founders.

Today, there are only a handful of religious colleges and universities in America that stand fast against the cultural decline and moral laxity that shapes American society. For that reason, in March 2017, I was invited to give a presentation about higher education to an organization of Catholic citizens in Chicago. I chose as my topic the decline of religious colleges. And since I was speaking to a Catholic audience, I focused on the decline of such Catholic colleges as the University of Notre Dame, Georgetown University, Loyola Marymount, Gonzaga, and Marquette. The commitment to the magisterium of the Church of all five has declined to the extent that concerned alumni have organized groups opposed to further decline.

My understanding of this social history is informed by two interesting books: *The Dying of the Light* (1998) by the late James Burtchaell[1] and a newer history, *From Christian Gentleman to Bewil-*

---

[1] James Burtchaell, CSC, *The Dying of the Light: The Disengagement of Colleges and Universities from their Christian Churches* (Grand Rapids, MI: William B. Eerdmans Publishing Co., 1998).

dered Seeker (2007) by Russell Nieli.[2]

The Dying of the Light examines representative colleges founded by Congregationalists, Presbyterians, Baptists, Lutherans, Catholics, and Evangelicals. When my reading progressed well into Chapter 6, entitled "The Catholics," I had to put the book aside. I had taught at the College of New Rochelle, a Catholic college where I had earned academic tenure. Burtchaell's description of the decline of that college was simply too depressing.

Russell Nieli's little book, *From Christian Gentleman to Bewildered Seeker*, examines American colleges and universities from their founding in the 1800s. All had a distinct religious character. Nieli observes that the first colleges were started by Protestant Christian denominations whose goal was to pass on to students the moral, intellectual, and religious heritage of Christianity and the culture of ancient Greece and Rome. Congregationalists, Presbyterians, and Anglicans were dominant and were followed in the 19th and 20th centuries by Methodists, Baptists, Lutherans, and other Protestant denominations.

Later, Catholics became active forming colleges for Catholic immigrants from Italy, and other southern and east European countries including Poland. These early institutions today are far removed from the ecclesiastical influences that shaped them as Christian institutions inspired by clerics and evangelists.

Among the institutions cited by Dr. Nieli are:

Harvard, Yale and Dartmouth—founded by New England Congregationalists.
Princeton—"New Light" Presbyterian
William and Mary, Columbia and Penn—founded by English Episcopalians

---

[2] Russell Nieli, *From Christian Gentleman to Bewildered Seeker: The Transformation of Higher Education in America* (Raleigh, NC: The John William Pope Center for Higher Education Policy, 2007).

Boston University; Northwestern Southern California, Syracuse, Vander-bilt—Wesleyan Methodist.

Brown and the University of Chicago—founded by northern Baptists *Georgetown, Fordham, and Notre Dame* were founded by Catholics.[3]

Even public colleges, Nieli observes, reflected the values of Protestant Christianity. These influences shaped the character and curriculum with compulsory morning Chapel and afternoon Matins, and courses that emphasized classical languages (Greek and Latin), Bible studies, and the ancient Greeks and Latin authors. Instructors were ordained clergy who were expected to teach a range of courses. The entire program of these institutions was dedicated to the service of Christ and the furtherance of moral and spiritual purposes.

During the 200 years between the European New England settlement of America and the American Civil War, Christian, that is, *Protestant,* education sought to combine the best in secular learning with the spiritual truths of the Bible. They were open to secular science and critical of the Catholic Church for its persecution of Galileo.

A turning point occurred with the American Civil War which, coupled with publication of Darwin's *On the Origin of Species* in 1859, shattered this world view. The Bible's explanation of Creation was challenged, and the brutality of the Civil War lessened Christian belief in a benevolent God. Also important, but little examined, American Transcendentalism imported German Idealism to America along with the Idealist view that man was essentially divine, thus challenging the Christian view of mortal man shaped in the image of God.

Many university scholars began studying in Germany and they

---

[3] Georgetown was not founded by Jesuits because on July 21, 1773, Pope Clement XIV suppressed the Society of Jesus. Georgetown's founding was in 1787.

clamored to adopt the practice of German research universities. Degree Programs and numbers of faculty were expanded and the concept of the unity of knowledge was challenged by academic specialization. In the 1870s, the "elective system" was gradually adopted and a common curriculum rejected.

Thus began what today we call "cafeteria style" education.

Dr. Nieli observes that education reformers "believed that it would be possible to combine the culture-and character-forming aspects of a Christian liberal arts college with the greater choice and opportunities it offered in a larger institution that conducted state-of-the art research... But their hopes proved to be illusion."

Gone was required chapel and the policy of hiring only committed Christians. Some scholars, including Irving Babbitt and John Erskine, were loudly critical, and Erskine introduced a core honors curriculum at Columbia University in the masterpieces of Western philosophy. That core curriculum remains today at Columbia, and another at the University of Chicago was founded by Mortimer Adler and Robert Hutchins. That core Great Books curriculum has many imitators even today.

But, then came the 1960s, the Free Speech movement, the anti-Vietnam war demonstrations, and demands that required courses be abolished. That was followed in the late-1980s and early 1990s by calls for multiculturalism to replace the emphasis on Western civilization. American higher education had entered an era of globalism, multiculturalism, and identity studies.

A changing America was one of the forces changing religious colleges, but also a dependency on U.S. government money was introduced by the Higher Education Act of 1965. According to "The Bennett Hypothesis," announced in a New York Time OpEd by then U.S. Secretary of Education, William Bennett, "Increases in financial aid in recent years has enabled colleges and universities blithely to raise their tuition, confident that Federal Loan subsidies would help cushion the increase."[4]

---

[4] William Bennett, "Our Greedy Colleges," *The New York Times*, Feb-

The Center for College Affordability and Productivity[5] estimated that over more than 30 years, between 1980 and 2012, college tuition increased 893% relative to an increase of 454% for healthcare and a 196% increase in the cost of food. Federal student loans increased to $1.292 billion in 2016 and the Wall Street Journal reported[6] that at least half of students who borrowed to pay tuition defaulted on those loans or failed to pay down loan balances over seven years. By 2019 "Lending Tree" estimated that direct student loans total $1.1503 trillion carried by 34.2 million borrowers. Of those 34.2 million borrowers, 11.5% of student loans are 90 days or more delinquent or are in default.[7]

This is accompanied by a growing lack of political diversity of college faculty. Between 1995 and 2010, according to the online Heterodox Academy, "...in the 15 years between 1995 and 2010 the academy went from leaning left to being almost entirely on the left."[8] Because in the Social Sciences and Humanities, the political orientation of most faculty is to the Left of center, even if required courses (dropped from most college curricula during the civil disturbances of the mid-1960s to early 1970s) returned, Leftist faculty would distort course content to suit their political disposition.

A cursory and unscientific review of which colleges continue a Western civilization core curriculum came up with only 21,[9] namely,

Traditional Liberal Arts
Hillsdale College

---

ruary 18, 1987.
[5] http://centerforcollegeaffordability.org
[6] *Wall Street Journal,* January 18, 2017.
[7] https://studentloanhero.com/student-loan-debt-statistics/
[8] http://heterodoxacademy.org/problems
[9]   See   https://www.collegeexpress.com/lists/list/great-books-colleges/240. CollegeExpress lists significantly more.

Western Civilization Programs
Texas Tech University
University of Houston

Christian Liberal Arts Colleges
Ave Maria University
University of Dallas
Campion College (Australia)
Biola University
Regent University
Liberty University
Wyoming Catholic
St. Bonaventure
Carthage College

Great Books
College of the Arts and Sciences (Internet)
St. John's College, Annapolis
St. John's College, Santa Fe
Thomas Aquinas College
College of St. Thomas More
Gutenberg College
University of St. Thomas
Mount St. Mary's University
Concordia University (Montreal, Canada)

This is a country with more than 4,000 colleges, many of which do not educate students in the history or culture of the West. In Australia, the late Paul Ramsay donated four billion dollars to establish a *Centre for the study of Western Civilization.* Most universities in Australia that offered new programs in the Great Books of the West rejected the offer.

In light of this curricular decline, we should not be surprised that free speech has been challenged on many American campuses and that many colleges have punished faculty who challenge the Politically Correct orthodoxy that dominates campus culture. According to "Campus Reform," an online project of The Leadership Institute, these same "Liberal" faculty donate exclusively to Democrat candidates.[10]

The loss of faith at Catholic colleges and universities where a theology of "Social Justice" has replaced Thomism is particularly grievous. Pope Leo XIII's encyclical, "Rerum Novarum[11] on the "Rights and Duties of Capital and Labor" promulgated in 1891 introduced concepts that would soon have a profound effect on the nature of American Catholicism. This encyclical affirms the right to own private property and affirms that private property is based in sacred laws of nature. And it asserts that the main tenets of socialism are contrary to the natural rights of mankind. That compels employers to duties that bind them to respect the dignity of workers. To misuse men as if they were "things," Pope Leo XIII says, is shameful. Recognizing that, the Church maintains associations for the relief of poverty.

The State also plays a role by assuring that the laws and institutions realize the public well-being and private prosperity. Inequalities of condition will always exist, but if morals are endangered by conditions in the workplace, if burdens placed on workers are unjust, and if health is endangered by excessive labor, it is right to seek the "aid and authority of the law." A dictate of natural justice requires that wages be sufficient to support "a frugal and well-behaved wage-earner." And Catholics who seek to better the condition of the working man are worthy of praise.

Forty years later, in 1931, Pope Pius XI issued the Encyclical *Quadragesimo Anno*[12] that went far beyond the ministrations of Pope

---

[10] https://www.campusreform.org/index.cfm?ID=8093

[11] http://w2.vatican.va/content/leo-xiii/en/encyclicals/documents/hf_l-xiii_enc_15051891_rerum-novarum.html

[12] http://w2.vatican.va/content/pius-xi/en/encyclicals/documents/hf_p-xi_enc_19310515_quadragesimo- anno.html

Leo XIII and affirmed concepts and ideas that intentionally rejected principles of economics that we associate with Adam Smith and free market capitalism.

Pius XI directly criticizes "individualism" and the Manchester school of economics and argues for an active government role in economic affairs. He objects to "inequality of wealth" and states the demands of "social justice." He relates social justice to the Common Good and argues [par. 109] that "free competition has destroyed itself; economic dictatorship has supplanted the free market; unbridled ambition for power has likewise succeeded greed for gain; all economic life has become tragically hard, inexorable and cruel."

By giving prominence to the dictates of social justice, Pius XI in *Quadragesimo Anno* inadvertently opened the door to the decline of interest in the philosophy of St. Thomas Aquinas and its replacement by a theology of "Social Justice." *Quadragesimo Anno* justified a transfer of focus of Catholic scholars from the pursuit of knowledge to the pursuit of political and economic action. That inclination to pursue salvation by means of political and economic action was reaffirmed on 15 May 1961 in *Mater et magistra*, the encyclical written by Pope John XXIII on the topic of "Christianity and Social Progress." A new theology of Social Justice had, thus, been granted Papal blessings.

My thesis requires a complete book and, in fact, one has been written by Thomas Patrick Burke, *The Concept Of Justice: Is Social Justice Just?*[13] Dr. Burke's essay entitled "The Origins of Social Justice: Taparelli d' Azeglio," published in *Modern Age*,[14] adds detail to this movement away from the pursuit of truth to social action.

That brings us to a Council of the Church, Vatican II, which met in 1962 about which Notre Dame Professor Ralph McInerny writes in *What Went Wrong with Vatican II* that Vatican II was not a

---

[13] Thomas Patrick Burke, *The Concept Of Justice: Is Social Justice Just?* (London: Bloomsbury Academic, 2013)
[14] *Modern Age*, Spring 2010 - Vol. 52, No. 2.

"basis for the postconciliar view ...that papal teaching can be legitimately rejected by Catholics."[15]

Ralph McInerny observed that after Vatican II, American Catholics experienced a discontent that led to flight from the priesthood and the religious life, liturgies that seemed bent on making the Mass a banal get-together, and a drive for "excellence" that displaced the teaching of Catholic doctrine.

As a graduate student at Notre Dame in 1965, I recall meeting a CSC novice at Notre Dame who told me that he wanted a secular education. Other students would ask, are we as good as Harvard? Today, that novice need not leave Notre Dame to receive a secular education, and my response to students at Notre Dame who asked if Harvard was "better" was "Notre Dame is better than Harvard."

At Vatican II, Pope John XXIII stated what he wanted the Council to accomplish: "that the sacred deposit of Christian doctrine should be guarded and taught more efficaciously.[16] Unfortunately, I believe, the outcome of Vatican II was tilted as early as 1931 by Pope Pius XI—not toward the Magisterium—but to an aggressive "Social Justice."

It gets worse.

I've read some pretty silly documents in my life, but the silliest is the Land O' Lakes Conference of 1967 where some twenty-five leaders of Catholic education signed a document entitled "The Idea of the Catholic University."[17] That document states that

a) "the Catholic university must have a true autonomy and academic freedom in the face of authority of whatever kind."

b) "the Catholic university is a community of learners...in which Catholicism is perceptively present..."

c) "theological investigation today must serve the ecumenical

---

[15] Ralph McInerny, *What Went Wrong with Vatican II: The Catholic Crisis Explained* (Bedford, NH: Sophia Institute Press, 1998).

[16] Ibid., 25.

[17] http://archives.nd.edu/episodes/visitors/lol/idea.htm

goals of collaboration and unity."

That requires that "theological or philosophical imperialism" be absent and the university should carry on a continual examination of all aspects...of the Church" and "will deal with problems of greater human urgency." The Land O' Lakes statement asserts that "the intellectual campus of a Catholic university has no boundaries and no barriers. "There must be no outlawed books." A Catholic university must be concerned with ultimate questions, interpersonal relationships, and pressing problems such as civil rights, peace, poverty. Students can learn by personal experience to consecrate their talent and learning to worthy social purposes.

No mention is made of the obligation of a Catholic university to teach Church history or the Magisterium of the Church and orthodox doctrine, nor does the document spell out what may make up a truly Catholic curriculum. So, in the face of this abandonment of a Catholic education by all major Catholic colleges and universities, what can be done?

One limited attempt at reform was made by Pope John Paul II's *Ex Corde Ecclesiae* promulgated on 15 August 1990. "From the Heart of the Church" holds that "every Catholic University, as *Catholic*, must have the following *essential characteristics:*

1. a Christian inspiration not only of individuals but of the university community as such;
2. a continuing reflection in the light of the Catholic faith upon the growing treasury of human knowledge, to which it seeks to contribute by its own research;
3. fidelity to the Christian message as it comes to us through the Church;
4. an institutional commitment to the service of the people of God and of the human family in their pilgrimage to the transcendent goal which gives meaning to life."[18] This re-

---

[18] Pt. I, *Apostolic Constitution of the Supreme Pontiff John Paul II on Catholic*

quires that "all Catholic teachers are to be faithful to, and all other teachers are to respect, Catholic doctrine and morals in their research and teaching. In particular, Catholic theologians, aware that they fulfill a mandate received from the Church, are to be faithful to the Magisterium of the Church as the authentic interpreter of Sacred Scripture and Sacred Tradition.[19]

Though its effect was limited, *Ex Corde Ecclesiae* cleared the air. Today, most "Catholic" colleges no longer qualify to call themselves "Catholic." If founded by religious orders, they refer to themselves as Jesuit, Benedictine, or Dominican.

Universities, 17.
    [19] Pt. II, *The University Community,* 50.

8.

Daimonic Souls and Recovery from Disorder

The ancient Greek philosopher, Plato, explains in *The Republic* that men live their lives as if they lived in a cave, hidden from light, where they can only see shadows. He adds that we are forced to turn around, however, and ascend to the light where we may see that reality which before we saw reflected in shadows (514a-517a).

Philosophy is the act of turning around and that turning around occurs when we comprehend a new truth about god: "The god is not the cause of all things, but of the good" (380c).[1] We thus find in Plato's philosophy a new critical insight into the relation of man to God, and the nature of divine reality. From this theological insight we may discover important ways to interpret the American regime.

I will be guided by Gerhart Niemeyer's discussion of this reality in *Between Nothingness and Paradise*, which explores the bond uniting a people in history. What is it that unites a people's past, its present, and the lives of those not yet born? What is this bond between political and social order and transcendent divine being that has been lost? For that, we must go back to the natural philosophers of ancient Greece who discovered "being" as the origin of "nature," especially Anaximander, who realized that being is divine.[2]

From the beginning of philosophy's break with cosmological myth, philosophers were conscious of experience of being (*to on*) as "mystic"—that which is beyond existing things (*ta onta*), or what is sometimes called nonobjective reality. St. Augustine expresses this mystic idea of order by means of a city in this world but not of this world; a city centered on Christ that is intertwined with a City of

---

[1] Plato, *The Republic of Plato*, Allan Bloom trans. (New York: Basic Books, 1968), 58.

[2] For an authoritative discussion of this discovery by Anaximander see Werner Jaeger, *The Theology of the Early Greek Philosophers.* (New York: Oxford Univ., 1967), 24-37.

Man lacking a divine center. Thus, the City of God has a common consciousness and experiences movement or peregrination of the soul leading to an end beyond the world. The City of Man has no end beyond this life and symbolizes the aimless social disorder of our age. How is this related to an American nation that continues in historical time? Unlike human beings, a society does not by its nature have a personal memory.

By analogy, Niemeyer writes, a society has a remembered past by reference to "a present unity of action" that is like the "identity of a person," except society "is not a natural substance. [A] society … is lacking this tangible phenomenon testifying to identity, the past alone is what could give identity to a society."[3] Society is a "created," not a natural, person. At the start, therefore, a society has no past, but over time materials of a historical past can be created into a consciousness of a historical past. An example that Niemeyer gives is that of ancient Israel:

> The fact is that the escapees from Egypt, when they finally stood in safety and freedom, experienced their deliverance as an act of God, an irruption of divine might into time and the affairs of men.[4]

How different was this experience of Israel's God from the gods of the other peoples of the ancient Near East?

One aspect of this difference was the awareness that the God of Israel was not a cosmic god. For millennia, mankind understood that man lived in a cosmos full of gods. Before the natural philosophers, Socrates and Plato broke with cosmic consciousness, the gods of the cosmos that shaped ancient man's understanding of the origin of the world and of empires.

Ancient Israel, distinguishable from the Greeks, interpreted its

---

[3] Gerhart Niemeyer, *Between Nothingness and Paradise* (Baton Rouge, LA: Louisiana State University, 1971), 145.
[4] Ibid., 155.

existence by remembering a one-time intervention by God in history. Niemeyer writes:

> A cosmological myth can be celebrated by reenacting again and again the story it relates. But an event that happened once in time and place, "before our eyes," even though experienced as a theophany, cannot be repeated or reenacted. God acted one time and his action can be only remembered.[5]
>
> Once the Exodus theophany had grown into the order of a people living under God on the strength of their public past, history had become a mold of human existence, as a model not only for 'Jacob and his sons' but for the entire human race.[6]

Consciousness of a public past deeply affects our present understanding, and there are some societies, such as Germany, that must confront the bad aspects of their past. Totalitarian movements in Europe after World War I left what some call a "dark past" of trauma that "cannot be assimilated or accepted."[7] The experience of German and Austrian scholars with Nazism led to a rejection of the political movements of that traumatic past.[8]

In this context, it is useful to consider that in modern Germany the word for "patriotic" has fallen into disuse because of the Nazi use of the term. It was, simply, too political, for German political theorists escaping political reality in political theory.[9]

That historical consciousness of life in nation-states defines the

---

[5] Ibid., 160.

[6] Ibid., 162.

[7] Anthony Polonsky and Joanna B. Michlic, eds., *The Neighbors Respond: The Controversy over the Jedwabne Massacre in Poland* (Princeton: Princeton University Press, 2004), 2.

[8] *The Collected Works of Eric Voegelin*, ed. Thomas Hollweck, vol. 30, *Selected Correspondence: 1950–1984* (Columbia: University of Missouri Press, 2007), 472.

[9] Eric Voegelin, *The New Science of Politics. An Introduction* (Chicago: University of Chicago Press, 1952).

West cannot be ignored. Consciousness of time–past, present and future–is a condition of Western human existence and challenges us to love our country.

Niemeyer writes, "Through its public past a community participates in the logos which remains the same in the flux of mutability; hence the community's identity imitates, as Boethius said, 'the ever simultaneous present immutability of God's life,' which is what one should rightly call eternal."[10] From this perspective, our nationhood as citizens of the United States, Niemeyer writes, "hinges on the all-important experience of a past at which a meeting occurred between time and eternity."[11] Consciousness of that history shapes our understanding of the life of the American nation: an understanding that can only be explained by myth.

Though it may seem improbable that the identity of modern America is shaped by myths, Niemeyer lists a number of truths we Americans affirm that are essentially mythic, including:

- We believe that individuals have souls;
- We proclaim an essential personal dignity and independence of mind;
- We distinguish time from eternity;
- We attribute authority to "the people" and to the "law";
- We affirm an enduring Constitution; and
- We affirm that we as a nation exist "under God."[12]

These myths do not depend on the consent of every American to their truth. Niemeyer suggests that the carriers of the truths of our myths may even be concentrated in a "remnant."[13] This recalls what Aristotle explained about right by nature. What is right can be

---

[10] Niemeyer, *Between Nothingness and Paradise*, 177–78.

[11] Ibid., 174.

[12] Ibid., 191.

[13] Ibid., 193.

known by mature men,[14] he said, and often we know it by reference to someone who knows what is right. In life we often ask ourselves, "What would he do?"

That he or she may be someone we know who can be relied upon for good advice. This is a powerful force in our private and in our public lives. These are persons who guide others in ways that can be political, moral, or simply "just." The reality of their presence in our lives is celebrated in art, literature, and film. For that reason, education from elementary to secondary school through college should aim to grow good character and replenish the numbers of mature, *daimonic*, men and women in each generation.

Niemeyer takes this essentially Aristotelian formulation and sharpens it with the assertion that:

> Christianity is the center of our culture, the truth that has shaped our past and is still shaping our present, regardless of what the attitude of particular persons to it may be. We cannot realistically step out of this truth into "another one," we cannot in truth become Hindus or Buddhists, and least of all can an amalgam be made of all religions as a dwelling place for anybody.
>
> Western civilization came into existence through the unifying impulse of Latin Christianity. No other religion has ever wielded a similarly powerful influence in the centuries of our cultural identity. The historical metamorphoses of our culture can be understood only in their relations to the Christian origins, even where these metamorphoses have not worked for but rather against Christianity.[15]

---

[14] Aristotle, *Nicomachean Ethics*, trans. Martin Ostwald (Indianapolis: Bobbs-Merrill, 1962). "Thus, what is good and pleasant differs with different characteristics or conditions, and perhaps the chief distinction of a man of high moral standards is his ability to see the truth in each particular moral question, since he is, as it were, the standard and measure for such questions" (1113a24). See also 1166a10, 1176a15, and 1176b20.

[15] Gerhart Niemeyer, "Christian Studies and the Liberal Arts College,"

At this late stage in the decline of the West, it is unlikely that consciousness of Christendom can be restored as a living force in civilization in the West. As Christianity ceases to be a living experience in the West, the historical consciousness central to the nature of Western nations diminishes. There is no modern Clovis to convert to Christianity, and the ancient tribes of Western Europe have consolidated into modern, secular nation-states. No modern "Great Awakening" is likely to occur, nor would it have lasting consequences were it to occur.

But there are restorative forces at work in every historical society, such as the experience of Yahweh that shaped ancient Israel, the discovery of the divine origin of nature in ancient Greece, the Gospels that shaped the Christian West after the fall of Rome, and in Confucian China and Hindu India, the insights of Confucius and Buddha.

Eric Voegelin writes, "The man who lives in the erotic tension to his ground of being is called *daimonios aner*, i.e., a man who consciously exists in the tension of the in- between (*metaxy*), in which the divine and the human partake of each other."[16] Aristotle's equivalent for the *daimonios aner* is the *spoudaios*, sometimes translated "mature man."[17]

Christian theology speaks of the reality of living in a state of grace. I think the concept "*daimonic*" explains not only Socrates' *daimon* but also the response of our souls to order in the face of disorder. It also is related to our anamnesis or recollection of the place or condition we existed previously. Before being born our souls existed in a world more real than the world we enter at birth. But our souls can remember that previous time and that recollection assists our becoming virtuous, of living in a state of grace.

We should not overlook, therefore, the presence of *daimonic*

---

in *The Loss and Recovery of Truth* (South Bend, IN: St. Augustine's Press, 2013), 511.

[16] Eric Voegelin, *Anamnesis*, Gerhrat Niemeyer trans. (Notre Dame, IN: University of Notre Dame Press, 1978), 154.

[17] Aristotle, *Nicomachean Ethics*, 1094a 19–26.

men and women who daily contend against the corrosion of civil society by ideological movements. These men and women are essential for renewal, for reducing the influence of political ideology on American life, and for recovery from cultural disorder.

Cultural conditions that foster good character are fragile, so we must ask if, at the end of the twenty-first century, there will be a vibrant, powerful, and spiritually healthy American nation?

Will we even remember the civilization of the Christian West?

Or will we suffer a loss of history and learn to accept bad economics, bad religion, failures in imperial foreign policy, and the uncertainty of a world of forces seeking to destroy our country?

Just as Plato saw that the best regime must affirm a new truth about God, if we interpret the American nation by reference to *esprit revolutionaire*—and not by reference to a philosophy that affirms our nation's participation in the divine ground and the force for good of *daimonic* men and women—ordered civil society will be abandoned for revolution.

In 2015, when I first suggested that social recovery can be found in the lives of *daimonic* men and women,[18] one reviewer noted that I had not mentioned the names of any of these *daimonic* souls. That misses my point that the presence in society of daimonic souls emulates the decision of Jesus to select fishermen as his disciples. The daimonic amongst us are plumbers, truck drivers, carpet layers, bank tellers. Only a few intellectuals, scientists, and corporation executives respond to their *daimon*. It would be impossible to "name names" since their numbers are legion and their collective action can be seen in their response to disorder in civil society.

---

[18] Richard Bishirjian, *The Conservative Rebellion*, 154-63.

9.

Conclusion

What can we conclude from this examination of the invasion in the corpus of Western culture by intellectual viruses of the French *philosophes*, idealist humanists of German idealism, and modern gnostics? Has our examination of these insights persuaded us that we citizens of the West need to recover from disorder?

Let's sum up this examination of *Conscience and Power* by examining aspects of Tocqueville's analysis of democracy in light of democracy in America today—almost two hundred years later.

A central aspect of that examination is the recognition that Tocqueville failed to develop an idea that he held deeply. In *Democracy in America*, he wrote: "The organization and the establishment of democracy in Christendom is the great political problem of our time" (183).

Tocqueville believed that the attack on religion in the French Revolution challenged the stability, order, and morality of democracy in France and was an attack on Christian religion. In *The Old Régime and the French Revolution*, he wrote, "By the 18th century Christianity had lost much of its hold on men's minds throughout Europe" and "in France, irreligion had become an all-prevailing passion..."[1]

Tocqueville's religious beliefs, however, were shattered by doubts fostered by the French *philosophes*, and though he was aware of that loss and its consequences for political order, he did not develop that subject directly. Other problems of democracy caught his attention, but we should not ignore this fundamental insight, even though Tcqueville didn't pursue it.

The contest for civilization in the West between conscience and

---

[1] Alexis de Tocqueville, *The Old Regime and the French Revolution*, trans. Stuart Gilbert (New York: Doubleday, 1983), 149.

power compels us to focus on these seven aspects of American political culture.

1. The attack on traditional order by the *philosophes*: Across the landscape of intellectual culture in the West, in print and electronic forms of communication, schools and universities, a political religion first formulated by French intellectuals in the 18th century and refined in German idealism of the 19th century now dominates our intellectual classes. Our colleges and universities are carriers of that political religion and, in the absence of required courses in traditional subjects, we have new curricula that defines a Left University. Just as the Spanish traditionalists sought to expel ideology of the French Revolution from Spanish universities, so it is incumbent on contemporary Europeans and Americans to address the problem of their Left Universities. The many wealthy businessmen, corporate executives, and successful high-tech professionals in the West have neglected higher education and placed their bets on candidates for political office.

    That is a fatal error.

    Their example should be the family of Leland Stanford who commemorated the death of his son by founding Stanford University in 1885. One hundred and thirty-eight years later, Stanford is a world class research university.

    It is not too late.

    Successful new colleges and universities can be created. Witness Liberty University founded by Jerry Falwell that claims 90,000 enrollments and Regent University founded by Pat Robertson which also has a robust online division.

    If the Coors Family, the heirs of Shelby Cullom Davis, the *nouveaux riche* Mercer family, the Templeton family or the Koch brothers followed the example of Jerry Fallwell or Pat Robertson and were to start a new university today, and staff it with scholars rooted in traditional scholarship, in fifteen to twenty years Mercer University or Koch, Cullom Davis, Templeton or Coors Universities would begin to compete for students with sectarian institutions like Liberty or Regent University and the many public universities in the United states.

And in England the example of Michael Oakeshott and Margaret Thatcher are a guide when they founded an independent University of Bukingham.

And, what if the very few American colleges that have a conservative "brand," such Hillsdale College, Grove City, or Pepperdine University, moved their "brand" across the nation in the way that John Sperling created Phoenix University? The cost of establishing such colleges in Los Angeles, Chicago, or New York is estimated at no more than five million dollars each, with all courses offered online. Moreover, abundant numbers of conservative scholars live, but are not employed as college teachers, in these major cities, and can be recruited to teach part or full-time. Instead, Hillsdale College, Grove City, and Pepperdine University continue in the tradition of one hundred years ago and build chapels, new campus buildings, and memorial walks.

2. Collusion of our legal classes with the administrative state: The Judicial power, Article III of the Constitution, and the literal words that make up the Constitution of the United States have been interpreted by the federal Judiciary to give itself—the Judiciary—a role in interpreting the Constitution. For that reason, some of the most difficult conflicts that have divided the nation have been decided, not by the resolution of contending interests through war or legislation, but by changing the meaning of the Constitution itself.

    In important ways, this changing of the meaning of the Constitution's words can affect the existential meaning of our common existence. When those changes are contrary to the original intention of the Framers, they constitute a severe and continuing problem for contemporary American politics.

We are now at that point.

The profession of law in the United States is pursued in law schools where the fundamentals of the practice of the law are taught to aspiring attorneys. Constitutional Law, however, is professed by legal scholars unappreciative of the philosophical basis of the Constitution.

The historical examination of the proceedings of the Philadelphia Convention and the Ratification Debates are ignored, and a Progressive interpretation of the class interests of the Founders is imposed. Thus, the Constitution, as it is taught in our law schools, is a document through which the powers of the administrative state grew and developed for the purpose of advancing "causes."

In our States constitutional officers, state Attorneys General, and judges who reflect this view of Constitutional law, dispose the States to become vassals of the national government. The only bright note that can be seen is the reduction in number of lawyers elected to the Congress of the United States in recent years. It may be hoped that the American electorate has discovered that a law degree is not a qualification for public service.

3. Mediocrity of our elected officials: Our elected officials are mediocre for the most part because since the late 1960s American colleges removed curricular requirements. Since 1973, students have not been educated in their responsibilities as citizens of a self-governing democracy. We have dumbed-down our college educated citizens and that may be seen in their faces that reflect vacant minds of elected officials.

Our First Amendment also protects the press that exposes details of the personal lives of persons seeking elective office. As a result, few qualified citizens are willing to subject their personal lives to press scrutiny. Thus, unlike the United Kingdom which has strict laws against libel, nothing is easier in the United States than to defame an elected official or candidate for office.

4. Growth of a centralized bureaucratic State. Despite warnings against concentration of power in the hands of one part of the government and the application of mechanistic principles of "balance," even the best intentions of the writers of the Bill of Rights and the Constitution of the United States could not deter the vice of centralization of power. Government agencies now service special interests and demands for greater welfare benefits.

    From the New Deal through subsequent programs of other American Presidents, a centralized bureaucratic administrative state has grown, and in growing its powers has chipped away at the individual freedoms of American citizens. Agencies of the national government examine every aspect of our lives and hold us hostage to edicts by non-elected officials. Neither party can be blamed for this: they are both culpable and seem unable to control what they collectively have wrought.

5. Usurpation of the powers of the States by the national government: the American States hold important powers that have been usurped simply by financing provided by the national government. No State official with good political sense will turn down federal largess. Thus, at this moment, over two hundred and thirty years since the Constitution was carefully drafted—and amended to reserve to the States powers not granted to the national government—nothing

of the original powers of the States remain that are not wa-
tered-down.

6.   Weakening of public customs and manners. Laws can only
     provide a basis for controlling powers of the administrative
     State. A necessary countervailing force has always been the
     common sense, traditional customs, religious faith, and
     good manners of the American people. Only the blind can-
     not see that very few of our good customs or manners re-
     main and the residue of common sense of the American
     people is being leached out of the fabric of our lives and
     civil society by our governing institutions.

7.   Demands for equality of condition that no laws can satisfy:
     Ideological demands are represented in every aspect of civil
     society. Racial minorities claim rights that may not be lim-
     ited. Sexual majorities (women) act as if they were minori-
     ties plagued by gender bias. Homosexual and transgender
     claims are made that cannot be legally denied. Even the
     rights of aliens to welfare and education benefits are confi-
     dently asserted and granted.

Many of these were concerns expressed by a 19th-century visitor
to the United States from France that forty years prior killed its
monarch and nobles, destroyed its churches and set its military
forces upon the world disrupting ancient regimes and sowing the
seeds of revolution into every part of Western Europe. What Alexis
de Tocqueville hoped was that American democracy was different.
And, indeed, when he wrote, America was different.

All that has changed.

My contemporary colleagues, Allan Bloom and James Piereson,
point out other problems.

Bloom's rejection of globalism, multiculturalism, and gender
studies reveals a colossal change in orientation of American colleges

and universities.

Studies in Western Civilization have been replaced by "globalism," as if we are now citizens of the world, first, and citizens of the United States last. To add insult to injury, religious colleges that should know better have joined the clamor for emphasis on non-Western—and non-Christian—studies. Some of that rejection of faith was led by religious "leaders," but, over time, parents of students no longer cared whether their students were educated in their religious faith so long as, after college, they got a good job or were admitted to law or medical school.

A pervasive relativism that afflicts American society was Bloom's gravest concern: "Values," Bloom writes, are a "new language of good and evil" designed to prevent us "from talking with any conviction about good and evil." This inability to face reality that the good can be known and that evil exists finds a compatible environment in "multiculturalism," which does not mean learning foreign languages nor learning about other cultures. It means acquiring the language of rejection of Western culture, traditions, and Christianity. Underlying this view is a form of relativism.

Multiculturalists insist that we change how we teach our children in order to reshape how they think. Specifically, they must stop thinking of Western and American civilization as superior to other civilizations. The doctrine underlying this position is cultural relativism—the denial that any culture can be said to be better or worse than any other. Cultural relativists take the principle of equality, which in the American political tradition is applied to individuals in terms of rights, and apply it instead to cultures in terms of their value.[2]

And pursuit of "identity studies" is simply another expression of loss of interest in substantive reality and leads to identity politics and the clamor for government redress of imagined grievances.

---

[2] Dinesh D'Souza, "Multiculturalism: Fact or Threat," *Imprimis* Volume 30, Number 9 (September 2001)

1 2 3

But these are concerns of educated elites, safely ensconced in Academe.

On the streets of America and in the bedrooms of our young, Rock, Rap, and other forms of popular music affect all Americans when they are most vulnerable. Captivated by excitement aroused by Rock musicians, early encounters with lyrics and melodies of popular music become reference points that chart moments in their personal lives. It is common for adult, educated Americans to identify the moment they first heard Led Zeppelin, or saw a video of Mick Jagger, as if that was a moment of spiritual grace.

Since these are moments of adolescent feelings, they might be expected to be replaced, as persons mature, by education in literature, classical music, Western thought or history, thus giving depth to their perceptions. Progression from feelings to ordered thought seldom occurs, however, thus a distinctive shallowness of American culture deepens and becomes clearer.

Can Bob Dylan be compared in the same breath to Giuseppi Verdi? Can the poetic skills in the compositions of T. S. Eliot or Allan Tate be compared to Bruce Springsteen—without laughter?

In August of 2017, North Carolina public television featured Peter, Paul and Mary's 2003 Carnegie Hall concert, as if this was something graduates of three world-class North Carolina Universities—the University of North Carolina, Wake Forest, or Duke University listening to UNCT—would find fulfilling.[3]

Why didn't the producers think of producing a reprise of the Wright Brothers based on David McCullough's compelling story of the birth of aviation at Kitty Hawk, North Carolina? That book had been published in 2015 and might have been used by Public Television in North Carolina to introduce an important moment of North Carolina and American history to a larger audience.

In other words, our people have been dumbed-down.

James Piereson looks for reforms in what Piereson calls a "Fourth Revolution" that reverses centralization of power. Thus,

[3] http://video.unctv.org/video/3003494159

we are left to look for signs that centralization of power in the national government and the powerful coalition of special interests and government are showing signs of an ending.

James Piereson outlines how that can occur by analysis of the principal theorist of government management of the economy, John Maynard Keynes. Revolutionary during his life, today we look askance at his view of a "system of capitalism in which large business enterprises and not-for-profit institutions operated alongside government in common efforts to promote the public interest."

The very words, "the public interest," today smack of a nanny state run by self-satisfied bureaucrats, smug foundation managers of "not-for-profits," and ill-educated accomplices in corporate America always looking for ways to appease the government. And might we not hope that these "leaders" will be shown the door?

But, by whom?

And here we return to a principal problem of democracy.

In democracies, all are equal, even the unequal, and seldom does leadership appear that turns this upside down world upright.

Our disappointment with Ronald Reagan, the best President in the last four decades, is deepened by the slovenly thinking of his Republican successors, not to mention the Presidents coughed up by Democrats. Clearly, "something has to give." But will whatever "gives" be salutary?

What are some changes that may occur?

We may soon see abolition of the Electoral College. If the popular vote is determinative, do we need an Electoral College?

If that occurs, we may see a realignment of the two Party system that will challenge how we elect members of Congress and contribute to the fragility of our Presidential elections.

And, then, there is the American military that has been granted increasing access to civilian power and the undisciplined minds of civilian officials. One day, American military leaders may decide that "enough is enough" and put a lid on "politics."

The future of democracy in the West in the short term does not look good. But over the long term, maybe in one hundred or more years, we may see a recovery that Alexis de Tocqueville, Francis Graham Wilson, Alan Bloom, and James Piereson prayed and hoped for.

Clearly, if there are articulate expressions of this hope, as surely there are, then there is, yet, even today, some evidence that we may meet the current crisis with a favorable ending.

Though corrupted, the citizens of Western democracies are not dumb, and they may tire of the decline of civilization in the West. Needless to say, our enemies in Russia, the People's Republic of China, Iran and in the cells of suicide bombers dedicated to Islam are watching what transpires.

When attacked, the citizens of Western democracies stand together. Just as the lives of American citizens were given new meaning during World War II when they learned something about themselves that they had not known, so we are assured that if we experience another attack, we all will stand together once again.

Let us hope that somewhere in some city, town, or village in the United States and in Europe there are possibly dozens of young persons living today who will have the virtue, character, wisdom, and will to lead their countrymen away from the dangers we now face

Appendices

Appendix A

Glossary of the Middle Ages

A

Abbey of St. Denis—Cathedral and burial site of French Kings, named after first Bishop of Paris martyred in 270 AD.

Abbot Suger of St. Denis (1081-1151)—French Abbot instrumental in developing Gothic architecture.

Alaric—King of the Visigoths, nomadic tribes of ancient Germans, who invaded Rome in 410 AD.

Albigensians—Manichaean sect known as Cathars who flourished in southern France.12th century.

Albigensian Crusade—ordered by Pope Innocent III in 1209 to exterminate the Cathars.

Alcuin (735-804)—English scholar, clergyman, poet, and teacher who was head of the school of York and assistant to Charlemagne

Alexius Comnenus (1057-1118)—Byzantine Emperor during the first crusade.

All Souls Day—Christian holiday celebrated to honor the souls of all deceased faithful Christians and, in Europe, All Souls Day is celebrated by visiting the graves of departed.

Angevin Monarchy (Plantagenets)—territories possessed by English kings, Henry II (ruled 1154–89), Richard I (r. 1189–99), and John (r. 1199–1216).

Anselm of Laon (d.1117)—founder of school at Laon that developed the study of biblical hermeneutics.

Augustus Caesar (63 BC - 14 AD)—Roman emperor who succeeded his uncle Julius Caesar. Caesar Augustus reigned when Jesus of Nazareth was born.

Augustine, Bishop of Hippo (354-430)—Catholic Saint—the

most influential of the early Fathers of the Church known for his defense of Christianity in his *City of God* and his *Confessions*.

Augustine of Canterbury (d. 604)—first Archbishop of Canterbury, responsible for establishing the Latin Church in England.

Arcadius (377-408)—Emperor of the Eastern Roman empire (395-408) and brother of Honorius who ruled the western Roman empire.

Arianism—the fourth century AD Christian heretic, Arius, sought to affirm the unity of God and asserted that Christ was not divine.

Averroes (1126-1198)—Islamic philosopher and advocate of Aristotle. Criticized for arguing that scripture should be interpreted allegorically when it contradicted reason.

Avicenna (980-1037)—Persian physician and thinker who developed a thought experiment by which a blind-folded man insensitive to space and time is still aware of his existence.

Aasil II (958-1025)—Byzantine Emperor, son of Emperor Romanos II and Empress Theophano, who destroyed the Bulgars and brought Antioch, Cyprus and Crete under Greek rule.

B

Basilica of Saint Denis—Cathedral in St. Denis (a suburb of Paris) completed in 1144 that was a forerunner of Gothic architecture. Burial site of French kings from the 10th to the 18th centuries.

Battle of Bouvines (1214**)**—concluding battle of Anglo/French war in which King Phillip Augustus of France defeated a coalition army of allies including King John of England. The defeat led to the signing of Magna Carta.

Battle of Civitate (1053)—defeat of Papal Army by Normans in southern Italy

Battle of Las Navas de Tolosa (1212)—King Alfonso VIII of Castile, Sancho VII of Navarre, Peter II of Aragon and Alfonso

II of Portugal defeated Muslim forces who controlled southern Spain.

Battle of Legnano (1176)—battle between Frederick Barbarossa, Holy Roman Emperor and king of Germany, and the Lombard League of cities in northern Italy centered in Milan. The Lombard League dealt a defeat to the Emperor.

Battle of Hastings (October 14, 1066)—-at village of Battle in what is now East Sussex, England, where the Norman duke, William, defeated Anglo-Saxon king Harold II. This defeat is called the Norman Conquest. Historians speculate that 2,000 Normans and 4,000 Englishmen were killed at Hastings, including King Harold.

Battle of Manzikert (August 1071)—battle between Seljuk Turks and Byzantine Empire near Manzikert Turkey. Defeat of Byzantine army led to Turkish control of Anatolia and Armenia.

Battle of Muret (1213)—battle between a Crusader army and Albigensians in Toulouse that destroyed the Cathars.

BCE—an abbreviation, used as early as 1708, for "before the Common (or Current) Era" as an alternative to the Anno Domini system ("in the year of the Lord"). Intended to express sensitivity to non-Christians.

Bede (672-735)—English monk at the monastery of St. Peter and its companion monastery of St. Paul at Jarrow in the Kingdom of Northumbria

Benedictines—provided the leadership of the 11th-century church

Benedict Biscop (c. 628-690)—founder of monastery and library of Jarrow in Northumbria

Bishop Ivo of Chartres (1040-1115)—Bishop of Chartres and a canonist who opposed King Philip I of France. A prolific writer, Ivo is known for advocating charity in propitiation for sins.

Bishop Otto of Freising (c. 1111-1158)—author of *The Deeds of Frederick Barbarossa*

Bishop Possidius (c. 437)—friend of St. Augustine exiled by King Gaiseric and present at Hippo upon the death of St. Augustine.

Blanche of Castile (1188-1252)—daughter of Alfonso VIII, King of Spain. Her son Louis became Louis IX and raised armies to subdue recalcitrant nobles.

Giovanni Boccaccio (1313-1375)—poet and author of *Decameron*, literally "Ten Days Work," that describes life during a plague that brings moral and social chaos; credited for his influence on Chaucer and Shakespeare.

Boniface (c. 672-754)—8th-century Christian who brought the Gospel to Germany and thus shaped Christianity in the West.

Bubonic Plague—carried to Messina in 1340, the largest city on Sicily, on twelve ships traveling from the Black Sea that spread a baccilus that killed 20 million Europeans. Boccaccio's *Decameron* describes the effects of the plague on society.

Jacob Burckhardt (1818-1897)—Swiss historian and scholar of the Renaissance

Byzantine Empire—founded by Roman emperor Constantine I in 330 AD on the site of the ancient Greek colony of Byzantium and intended as a continuation of the Roman Empire besieged by invading German tribes.

C

Cardinal—Latin word for the "hinge" of a door.

Humbert of Silva Candida (c. 1000-1061)—French Cardinal who excommunicated the Patriarch of Constantinople in 1054 thus originating the "Great Schism" between the Roman church and Eastern Orthodox.

Carthage—originally a Phoenician city located in present day Tunisia. Destroyed by the Romans in 146 BC.

Carthusians—monastic order founded in 1084 and named after the Chartreuse Mountains in the French Alps near Grenoble. Known for rules called "Statutes" and a liquor or cordial, Chartreuse, made by monks since 1737.

Cathars—heretical sect that advocated a Gnostic dualism of a good

God who created spiritual life and an evil God who created material reality.

Carolingian Empire—ruled by Frankish kings from 800-888 founded by Charlemagne.

Capetian monarchy—French dynasty founded by Hugh Capet (987) through the end of the reign of Charles IV (1328).

Celtic Church—distinguished by devotion to learning and missionary zeal; declined after 800 AD and ceased to play an important role in European cultural life

Champagne Fairs—one of the earliest manifestations of a linked European economy, a characteristic of the High Middle Ages.

The Church—derived from the Greek word "ecclesia" or assembly. The early Christians considered themselves members of The Church.

Charles the Bald (823–877)—King of West Francia (843–877), King of Italy (875–877) and Holy Roman Emperor (875–877)

Charles Martel (686-741)—victor over Moslems in 732 at Tours.

Charlemagne (742-814)—king of the Franks and later king of the Lombards (northern Italy), eldest son of Pepin II. Crowned by Pope Leo III as Emperor of the Romans, improved church discipline and further education in the monastic schools.

Christ—"One anointed by God"

City of God—concept conceived by St. Augustine to indicate that history is not simply the story of the rise and fall of empires. There is a greater city that lives throughout history and is made up of citizens who love God. Their pilgrimage toward salvation is the greater history of the City of God.

Cistercians—monastic order founded around 1110 by Benedictine monks seeking to literally follow the Rule of St. Benedict centered on manual labor and self-sufficiency.

Clovis (466-511)—conqueror of Gaul, king of the Franks and founder of the Merovingian dynasty. Claimed that "the entire kingdom was the property of his family."

Concordat of Worms of 1122—treaty between Pope Calixtus II and Henry V that recognized the King as having the right to invest bishops with secular authority in the territories they governed, but not with sacred authority .

Confessions—a method of reflection by which sins are confessed and forgiveness granted. St. Augustine's "Confessions" are a major contribution to our understanding of how Christians repent. Later confessions, such as that of Jean-Jacques Rousseau, were transformed into expressions of self-love.

Conrad IV (1228-1265)—son of Frederick II and heir to the Crusader State of Jerusalem. Died from malaria at age 29.

Constantine the Great (c. 280-337)—proclaimed Emperor in 306 AD. In a battle with Maxentius, governor of Rome in 312 AD, Constantine experienced a vision that he should conquer Rome in the name of Christ. He was victorious and Constantine decreed that Christian worship would be tolerated.

Constantinople—founded by Constantine the Great in 324 AD on the site of ancient Byzantium, Constantine declared Constantinople (present day Istanbul) as the new capital from which he would rule the Roman empire.

Council at Clermont (1095)—convoked by Pope Urban II to attract knights to participate in First Crusade, promised plenary indulgences for their sins.

Council of Nicaea—Convened by Constantine in 325 AD, this council of Christian bishops affirmed the theology of Christ as Son of God and other theological principles of the early Church. A version of the Nicene Creed is recited in Catholic, Lutheran, Episcopal, and other Christian churches in the present day and is a singular statement uniting all Christians.

First Crusade (1095)—called by Pope Urban II to help reunite Christendom, enhance papal prestige, make the Byzantine emperor subservient, and provide French feudal princes and knights opportunities for conquest.

Second Crusade (1144)—preached by St. Bernard of Clairvaux in response to calls for assistance by the Latin Kingdom. Persuad-

ed Louis VII of France and Conrad III of Germany to participate.

Third Crusade (1190)—participating were Richard the Lion-
hearted of England, Philip Augustus of France, and Frederick
Barbarossa of Germany.

Fourth Crusade (1204)—preached by Pope Innocent III was directed against Byzantium and conquered Constantinople.

Crusader State of Jerusalem—Christian state established in 1099
after the first Crusade on territory of modern-day Israel, Jordan,
and the West bank and Gaza of contemporary Palestine.

D

Damascus—capital of Syria, approximately 178 miles from Jerusalem. Famous for Saul's encounter with Christ on the road to
Damascus.

Herbert Deane (1921-1991)—Columbia University professor of
political philosophy notable for his work on St. Augustine.

The Decalogue—the "Ten Commandments" inscribed by God on
two tablets given to Moses on Mt. Sinai

Denarius—silver coin consisting of 240 parts of one pound of silver in Constantine's monetary system

Desmesne—lands of an estate

Diocletian (c. 245-316)—proclaimed Emperor of Rome in 284
AD, Diocletian governed an empire endangered by Visigoth
tribes that ultimately destroyed Rome. Attempting to ensure his
authority, Diocletian persecuted Christians and revived worship
of Rome's ancient gods.

Domesday Book—compiled by order of King William and completed in 1086 to determine what taxes had been owed during
the reign of King Edward the Confessor. Provided a complete
record of wealth and landholders.

Dominicans—Approved by Pope Honorius III in 1216 to preach
the Gospel and to oppose heresy, also known as the Order of

Preachers, the philosopher of the Church, St. Thomas Aquinas, was a Dominican.

Donation of Constantine—an 8th century forged decree of 4th century Emperor Constantine used to support claims of authority over Rome and the western part of the Roman Empire by the Pope.

Donation of Pepin—a grant in 751 to Pope Stephan by King Pepin extending to the Pope territories beyond Rome.

Donatism—a Christian sect in Roman Africa (present day Algeria and Tunisia) that flourished in the 4th and 5th centuries. Donatists held priests to high ethical standards if their prayers and sacraments were to be effective.

E

Edward the Confessor of England (1003-1066)—restored English rule of the House of Wessex after the invasion of Danes in 1016. The Battle of Hastings (1066) established Norman governance under William the Conqueror.

Edward I (1239-1307)—son of Henry III, defeated English barons in the Second Baron War (1265) and participated in the Ninth Crusade. Crowned King in 1274.

Eleanor of Aquitaine (1122-1204)—married Louis VII of France and participated in the Second Crusade. Her marriage was annulled in 1152. She then married King Henry II of England. Her second son, Richard the Lionheart became King of England and acted as Regent when King Richard went on the Third Crusade.

F

First Europe—a new distinct culture and society formed between 750 and 900 in Western Europe, coextensive with the area of Latin Christianity and consisting of a confluence of Germanic culture and Latin-Christian culture. "First Europe" included France, England, western Germany, Ireland, northern Italy, and northern Spain.

Frankish Monarchy— *"Frank"* was a synonym for *Western European*, governed by Carolingian Franks who ruled most of civilization in Western Europe that was the basis of the European political order until the French revolution.

Frederick I (1122-1190)—elected King of Germany in 1152 and crowned Roman Emperor by Pope Adrian IV in 1155.

Fulda Monastery—founded by St. Sturmi, a disciple of St. Boniface, in Fulda (contemporary State of Hesse) in 744 and burial site of St. Boniface.

Franciscans—monastic order established in 1209 by St. Francis of Assisi.

Fourth Lateran Council—convoked in 1215 and defined Transubstantiation.

Frisia—A coastal region along the southeastern corner of the North Sea in what today is mostly a large part of the Netherlands, homeland of the Frisians, a Germanic people.

G

Gaul—a region of Western Europe during the Iron Age that was inhabited by Celtic tribes, encompassing present-day France, Luxembourg, Belgium, most of Switzerland.

Gelasian doctrine—letter by Pope Gelasius I establishing that secular authority was inferior to priestly spiritual authority but that spiritual authority in matters secular was inferior to secular authority.

Geoffrey of Monmouth (1095-1155)—English cleric possibly born in Monmouth, Wales, and author of *The History of the Kings of Britain* (c.1136) and expositor of the legend of king Arthur.

Gaiseric—King of the Vandals who moved his tribe from Andalusia, Spain, to north Africa and destroyed the Eastern and Western Roman empires in 430 AD. His forces occupied the city of Hippo as St. Augustine lay dying.

Gelasius I (d. 496)—Pope from 492-496 AD asserted the doctrine of the "two swords."

Gerbert of Aurillac (c. 946-1003)—renowned scholar, counselor to Otto III and Pope Sylvester II from 999-1003

Germanic invasions (c. 300-425)—sometimes called the Germanic wars or the "migration period" represent movement of Germanic tribes into Roman territory. In Rome's decline, Rome's outer defenses were diminished and led to the fall of Rome itself.

Giotto di Bondone (1267-1337)—painter of frescoes in Assisi, Rome, Naples, Florence.

Gregory I, the Great (c 540-604)—Pope from 590-604 AD provided for the poor of Rome and spread Christianity to Britain and the German tribes.

Gregory of Tours (538-594)—historian and Bishop of Tours. Author of History of the Franks.

Gregory VII (1015-1085)—born "Hildebrand." As Pope Gregory VII created the Investiture Controversy. Excommunicated emperor Henry IV, an act that shook the foundations of western society.

Gregory IX (1227-1241)—successor of Innocent III

Ghibelline and Guelphs—factions in Italian city states of 12th and 13th centuries. The Ghibelline faction supported the Holy Roman Empire and the Guelphs supported the Pope.

H

Henry I, the Fowler (c. 876-936)—duke of Saxony, a northern Duchy of Germany, elected king in 918

Henry II (973-1024)—successor of Otto III of Germany

Henry II of England (1133-1189)—also known as Henry Plantagenet. Controlled England, Scotland, parts of Ireland and

France in what is called the Angevin Monarchy.

Henry III (1016-1056)—became King of Germany in 1039 and was crowned emperor by Pope Clement II in 1046.

Henry IV (1105-1106)—German emperor, forced to abdicate in 1105, excommunicated three times during the Investiture Controversy

Henry V (1081-1125)—renounced right of investiture in Council of Worms, 1122

Henry VI (1165-1197)—a Hohenstaufen King of Germany and Holy Roman Emperor

Henry of Bracton (c. 1210-c.1268)—an English cleric and jurist

Hippo Regius—major Christian city in ancient Roman Africa now the present day Annaba in Algeria

Hohenstaufen—dynasty of German kings that ruled the Holy Roman Empire from 1138 to 1208 and from 1212 to 1254. Located in southern German region of Swabia that included Tübingen, Stuttgart, and parts of Bavaria and the regions of Alsace and Baden in the Upper Rhine Valley.

Holy Roman Emperor—a title conveyed upon Charlemagne by Pope Leo III in 800 AD that proclaimed primacy of German kings from 800 to 1806.

Hugh Capet (939-996)—elected in 987 the first King of the Franks of the House of Capet, a powerful landed family in the Île-de-France.

Hugh the Great (1024-1109)—Abbot at Cluny, driving force behind the Cluniac monastic movement during the last quarter of the 11th century.

I

Innocent III (c.1160-1216)—powerful Pope who claimed supremacy over kings of Europe. Presided over the Fourth Lateran Council that dealt with transubstantiation, papal primacy, and the conduct of clergy.

Investiture Controversy—controversy begun in 1056 when a church council declared that the power of investiture lay with the church. Pope Gregory VII in 1076 excommunicated Emperor Henry IV for his investiture of the Bishop of Milan. A famous meeting at Canosa Castle in Reggio nell'Emilia with Henry IV defined this controversy with the title "walk to Canosa."

Innocent IV (1195-1254)—clashed with Emperor Frederick II who hoped the new Pope would revoke his excommunication. At a general council in Lyon in 1244, Innocent IV deposed Frederick II.

Île-de-France—geographic region in France around Paris.

Islam—monotheistic religion teaching that there is only one God and that Muhammad is the messenger of God

J

Jarrow—school and library in Northumbria destroyed by Vikings in 8th century

John Scotus Eriugena (815-877)—an Irishman in the court of Charles the Bald who translated the Neoplatonic works of Dionysius

John of Salisbury (1120-1180)—a student of Peter Abelard at the University of Paris and secretary to the Archbishop of Canterbury and became bishop of Chartres in 1173. Author of Policraticus.

K

Knights Templar—Catholic military order founded in 1119 that attracted nobles seeking to recover the Holy Land. Disbanded in 1312.

L

Life Eternal—aspiration, from the Greek word *athanatos*, to be deathless, and central to Christ's promise of eternal life to those who believed and kept God's commandments.

Lanfranc (1005-1089)—foremost theologian of mid-11th century; archbishop of Canterbury (1070–89) and counselor to William the Conqueror.

Lateran Councils—Catholic councils held in the Lateran Palace in Rome.

Latin Kingdom of Jerusalem—established at Ascalon after first crusade in 1099 and settled by French crusaders. The city of Jerusalem was lost in 1187 and the Latin Kingdom was extinguished in 1291.

Lombards—German tribe located in Austria and Slovakia in the 5th century that invaded Italy in late 569 AD.

Lombard League (1167)—alliance supported by Pope Innocent III to counter the influence in Italy of the Hohenstaufen Holy Roman Emperors.

Lordship—basis of social and institutional order of Germanic society

Louis the Pious (814-840)—son of Charlemagne.

Louis VI the Fat (1081-1137)—King of France who consolidated his power over French nobles and managed the wedding of his son, Louis VII to Eleanor of Aquitaine.

Louis VIII (1187-1226)—led crusade against Albigensians

Louis IX (1214-1270)—contemporary of St. Thomas

M

Magna Carta—charter of liberties granted by King John to English barons on June 15, 1215, at Runnymede.

Maimonides (c. 1135-1204)—Sephardic Jewish philosopher, contemporary of Averroes.

Manichean—a religion of the third century AD that explained the origin of evil as the attempt by an evil Demiurge to capture the light of the good God. Salvation defined as escape of the light from darkness was attained through secret knowledge (gnosis).

Merovingian Dynasty—a kingdom of Franks founded by Merovech whose son, Clovis, unified Gaul.

Messiah—from the Greek word "Christos" —"anointed one"

Michael Oakeshott—English political theorist who championed conservative political ideas and with Margaret Thatcher founded a private University in the belief that English higher education in England was too much controlled by the state.

Missi—representatives of Charlemagne sent on periodic tours of inspection to affirm control over local royal officials.

Moslem Conquest—from 711 to 788, the Umayyad Caliphate expanded into Iberia, expelling the Visigoths.

Muslim—someone who follows or practices Islam; Muslim majority countries are Indonesia, Pakistan, Egypt

N

Neo-Platonism—Ancient Greek philosophy was continued by Neo-Platonists, namely Plotinus (c. 204/5-270), whose influence on St. Augustine shaped early Christian theology.

Nero (37-68)—Roman Emperor known for persecution of Christians

Norman Cohn (1915-2007)—British historian and author of *Pursuit of the Millennium*; demonstrated that totalitarian ideologies were similar to Medieval apocalyptic movements such as the Flagellants and the Anabaptists.

O

Odilo of Cluny (962-1049)—actively worked to reform the monastic practices at Cluny and at other Benedictine houses. He also promoted the Peace of God movement.

Otto I (936-973)—son of Henry I, creator of the German monarchy; elected king in 936

Otto II (955-983)—killed fighting the Moslems in southern Italy in 983

Otto III (983-1002)—acceded to throne as a child; empire ruled until 995 by a regent, Otto's mother, Theophano.

Ottonian Dynasty—a Saxon dynasty of German monarchs (919–1024)

P

Paschal II (c. 1050-1118)—last of four Gregorian Popes distinguished for their reforms.

Peace of God Movement—late 10th century attempt by the church to protect ecclesiastical property, including relics of saints, and personnel

Pepin II (635-713)—leader of the Carolingians in France and "Duke of the Franks." Son of Charles Martel. "Anointed" by St. Boniface thus introducing the principle of "theocratic monarchy."

Pepin III (Pepin the Short) (714-768)—sole *de facto* ruler of the Franks in 747 and father of Charlemagne

Peter Abelard (1079-1142)—12th-century scholastic theologian. Consort of Heloise, a French nun who became Abelard's lover.

Peter Damiani (c. 1007-c. 1072)—Cardinal and Benedictine monk in circle of Pope Leo IX, introduced more severe monastic disciplines including flagellation and attempted to reform clergy in northern Italy.

Petrine theory—doctrine on primacy of the Roman pontiff based on Christ's bestowing the "keys of the Kingdom" on St. Peter.

Philip I (1052-1108)—Capetian king of France, excommunicated twice, the second time by Pope Urban II for abandoning his wife and marrying the wife of the Count of Anjou.

Philip II Augustus (1165-1223)—king of France following in a line of King of the Franks. Victorious at the Battle of Bouvines (1214).

Plantagenets—royal family that held the English throne from 1154, with the accession of Henry II, until 1485, when Richard III died.

Policraticus (1159)—John of Salisbury's "advice" to kings.

R

Ravenna—capital city of the Western Roman empire in 402 AD

Rodrigo Díaz de Vivar (c. 1043-1099)—"El Cid" or "Lord." A Castilian nobleman who has become a Spanish folk-hero celebrated for his military achievements.

Robert Grosseteste (1170-1253)—Scholastic philosopher and theologian credited for establishing Oxford as a center of science in Medieval England.

Roger Bacon (1219-1292)—Franciscan friar, philosopher, and student of nature. Groundbreaking student of mathematics, optics, alchemy, and astronomy.

Roscelin of Compiègne (1050-1125)—"Nominalist" who held that what we know are words, not things themselves.

S

Salian Dynasty, successor to Ottonian Dynasty, also known as Frankish Dynasty of Franconia

St. Ambrose (c. 339-c. 397)—fourth century AD Bishop of Milan. Defender of the Church against heretical Arianism.

St. Anselm (1033-1109)—archbishop of Canterbury, successor of Lanfranc, known for the celebrated "ontological argument" for the existence of God in the *Proslogion*.

St. Augustine (354-430)—the most influential of the early Fathers of the Church known for his defense of Christianity in his *City*

of God and *Confessions.*

St. Bernard of Clairvaux (1090-1153)—Benedictine who was instrumental in founding the Cistercian Order. Founded a monastery in *Claire Vallée,* between Lake Geneva and Mont Blanc in the French Alps in *1115.*

St. Benedict of Nursia (480-c. 547)—formulated the "Rule of St. Benedict" used by Benedictine for 15 centuries and considered the founder of Western Christian monasticism

St. Benedict of Aniane (747-821)—placed at head of Carolingian monasteries by Louis the Pious, son of Charlemagne

St. Bonaventura (1221-1274)—Franciscan and a fellow student of St. Thomas at the University of Paris and developed the Franciscan order to preeminence.

St. Boniface (675-754)—missionary to the Franks and named Archbishop of Mainz and martyred in 754

St. Columban (543-615)—Irish missionary who preached a monastic rule of penitential practices, confessions to a priest and penances.

St. Francis of Assisi (1181-1226)—Influential Italian friar who in 1209 founded the Franciscan Order soon followed by the women's Franciscan Order, the Order of Saint Clare, and a lay order, Third Order of Saint Francis.

St. Paul (c. 5-c 64/65)—first known as "Saul of Tarsus," a persecutor of Christians, converted to Christianity in a mystic encounter with the living Christ on travel to Damascus and spread the Gospel of Christ to non-Jews.

St. Thomas (1225-1274)—born near the village of Aquino in Italy, thus, commonly, but incorrectly, called "Aquinas." St. Thomas is honored as a Father of the Church. His writings include disputations, philosophical commentaries, systematic works (the *Summa Theologiae* and *Summa contra Gentile),* commentaries on books of the Bible and Liturgical works, letters and Tractates.

Sic et Non—list of propositions and counterpropositions by Peter Abelard.

Siger of Brabant (1240-1284)—philosopher from the Netherlands and advocate of the 12th-century Islamic philosopher Averroes, murdered in Orvieto in southwest Umbria.

Simon de Montfort (c. 1208-1265)—leader of the Albigensian crusade

Seljuk Turks—Sunni Muslim dynasty that extended from Anatolia to Iran and was the object of the First Crusade; remembered as great patrons of Persian culture, art, literature, and language.

T

Theodore of Tarsus (602-690)—scholar who established an influential school of learning at Canterbury.

Theodosius the Great (347-395)—Roman emperor from 379 to 395 AD. Declared Christianity the official church of the Roman empire.

Thomas Stearns Eliot (1888-1965)—American poet and author of *The Wasteland* who explored the relation between religion and literature.

Thomas Beckett (1119-1170)—Archbishop of Canterbury who defended the rights and privileges of the Church in opposition to King Henry II of England. Murdered in Canterbury Cathedral by followers of the King.

Trappists—a monastic order, officially the Order of Cistercians of the Strict Observance named after La Trappe Abbey in Soligny-la-Trappe, Orne, in Normandy France about 83 miles from Paris.

Treaty of Verdun (843)—partition of the Carolingian empire by the sons of Louis the Pius.

Three Wise Men—the "Magi"—educated men who came seeking the Christ child.

U

Urban II (1035-1099)—Pope who succeeded Gregory VII and enhanced papal prestige.

Umayyad Caliphate—one of four Caliphates formed after the death of Muhammad.

V

Virgil (70-19 BC)—Roman poet, author of the *Eclogues*, the Georgics, and the *Aeneid*.

Viking marauders—a consequence of struggles in Denmark and Norway that led to defeated warrior bands invading the river valleys of western Europe, ports in Italy and northern France

Visigothic Spain—a kingdom of Visigoths that occupied what is now southwestern France and the Iberian Peninsula from the 5th to the 8th centuries.

W

William the Conqueror (c. 1028-1087), also known as William II, the Bastard, before his conquest of England. Most powerful king in Europe after decline of the Salian (Franks) monarchy.

Appendix B

Historical Timelines

Ancient Israel

Moses (c. 1391 BC)—Revelation of Yahweh Ancient Israel occupies Canaan

Israelites fight the Philistines (c. 1150 BC) Assyrians (740 BC) destroy northern Israel Isaiah (740 BC)—chastises Israel

Jeremiah (626 BC)—prophesies Babylon's capture of Israel

Babylonian Captivity—Forced Detention (587 BC) King Herod (74 BC)—client ruler of Roman Palestrina

Ancient Rome to Birth of Jesus

Rome unites the Italian peninsula (fourth and third centuries BC)

Punic Wars (264 BC - 146 BC) Three Wars between Rome and Carthage Rome destroys Carthage (contemporary Tunis) 146 BC

Polybius (c. 200 – c. 118 BC), *The Histories* attributes Rome's success to a "Mixed Constitution"

Rise and Fall of the Roman Republic (509 BC-27 BC)

Cato the Elder (234 BC–149 BC) Conservative Roman soldier, senator, and historian known who opposed Hellenization and ended his speeches *Carthago delenda est* (Carthage must be destroyed)

Publius Cornelius Scipio Africanus (236/235-c. 183 BC)—defeated Hannibal at the Battle of Zama in 202 BC

Cicero (106 BC-43 BC), lawyer, senator and philosopher

Marcus Porcius Cato, "Cato The Younger" (95 BC-46 BC)—a Stoic, contra Caesar

Pompey (Gnaeus Pompeius Magnus) (106 BC - 48 BC)

Gaius Julius Caesar (100 BC-44 BC) – Roman general and statesman

Battle of Actium (31 BC) – the location of Octavius Caesar's defeat of Mark Antony

Ancient Greece

Greek tribes conquer the Greek mainland and islands
Trojan war and sack of Troy (1194 – 1184)
Sparta waged war against the city of Troy/Paris of Troy took Helen
    from her husband, Menelaus, king of Sparta.
Homer (c. 8th century BC)—Illiad & Odyssey
Hesiod (c. 750 BC)—Theogony & Works and Days
Solon (c. 630-c.560 BC) becomes Archon of Athens in 594 BC
    (admired by the Founders)
Cleisthenes (570 BC-508 BC) introduces democratic reforms
    (508/7 BC)
Greeks populate colonies throughout the Mediterranean
"Great Age" of Pericles (c. 495-429 BC)—rules Athens c. 457 BC
Aeschylus (c. 525-455 BC)—Suppliants & Oresteia
Euripides (c. 480-406 BC)—Medea & Iphigene in Aulis
Thucydides (460-c. 395 BC)—History of the Peloponnesian War
Herodotus (450-420 BC)—The Histories
Sophocles (497-406 BC)— Oedipus Rex, Antigone, and Oedipus at
    Colonus
Socrates (469-399 BC)—Plato's teacher
Xenophon (c. 430-354 BC)—Anabasis, Memorabilia & Apology

Wars & Disorder in Ancient Greece

Peloponnesian War (431-404 BC)
Sparta prepares to destroy Athens in league with other Greek cities
Peace of Nicias (421 BC)—six years of peace
Athens defeated at Syracuse (413 BC)
Rule of the Four Hundred (411 BC)—overthrow of Athenian de-
    mocracy Surrender of Athens (404 BC)
"Thirty Tyrants" Pro-Spartan oligarchs govern Athens
Socrates sentenced to death (399 BC)
Second Athenian League—Athenian political union (378-355 BC)

Plato (c. 428-328 BC)
Aristotle (c. 384-322 BC)

Christianity: From Persecution to State Religion

Caesar Augustus (63 BC-14 AD)
King Herod (73 BC-4 BC)
John the Baptist (c. 1st century BC-c. 30 AD)
Baptism of Jesus of Nazareth
Nero (37-68 AD)
Christian Persecutions
Execution of St. Peter (d. between 65-68)
Execution of St. Paul (d. between 64-65)
Marcus Aurelius (161-180)
Diocletian (244-312)
Constantine (272-337)
Christianity made the official state religion (380 AD)
Alaric invades Rome (410 AD)

The Early Christian Era

By the end of the 5th century AD, "barbarian" tribes ruled all of
    Italy, but as Rome was felled by invaders, there arose the suc-
    cessors to St. Peter, Bishops of Rome, who eked out a spiritual
    space independent from emperors governing "the state" and,
    ultimately, converted the invaders to Christianity.

Conversion to Christianity of the invading tribes affirmed a moral
    order that became the hallmark of Western civilization. That is
    central to Christian civilization in the West.

The continuity of that order from classical antiquity to what is
    called the Middle Ages was maintained by the Church.

Two Popes of the early Church were central to the rise of a Chris-
    tian Civilization Gelasius I, died 496 AD—doctrine of the
    "Two swords"

Gregory the Great (540 AD-604 AD)—converted German tribes to
Christianity and made Rome the spiritual center of the West

Appendix C

How Music Corrupts Billboard's "Best Singles"

Allan Bloom reminds us that Plato took music seriously and believes that we should, too.

In Plato's *Republic*, the discussants seeking to know what is the best regime agree that music should be taught first, even before gymnastics (376e). Censorship is an aspect of the best city developed in Plato's *Republic*, and music is not exempted.

Music that is permitted will exclude "wailing and lamentations" (398e),[1] but harmonic modes are allowed. Only the rhythms of an orderly and courageous life are permitted (399e).

This Appendix samples Billboard's Best Singles in 1942, 1952, 1957, 1965, 1968, 1972, 1973, and 2016.[2]

Very few of these "best" singles would be acceptable in Plato's best regime, nor even Allan Bloom's Chicago of 1987, yet a significant change in music from 1942 is evident in the year 1957 when the "Number 1" single was Elvis Presley's "All Shook Up."

In 1942, traditional melodies sung by vocalists such as Bing Crosby and arrangements by Jimmy Dorsey, Glenn Miller, and Harry James were followed in the 1950s by Kay Starr, Vera Lynn, Rosemary Clooney, and Eddie Fisher.

Even twenty-three years later, in 1965, older popular tastes are reflected in Don McLean's "American Pie," Sammy Davis, Jr.'s "Candy Man," and the Beatles "Help." In 1968, we see the Beatles' "Hey Jude" and Simon and Garfunkel's "Mrs. Robinson," and in 1972 and 1973 Roberta Flacks's "The First Time Ever I Saw Your Face" and "Killing me Softly" are #1 and #3. All are songs and melodies that charm us even today.

---

[1] Allan Bloom, trans., *The Republic of Plato* (New York: Basic Books 1968), p. 77.

[2] Copyright © http://billboardtop100of.com.

Comparing them to Justin Bieber's two hits in 2016, "Love Yourself" and "Sorry," suggests the arrival of another music audience—younger, wealthier, and challenged by the absence of accepted music standards and with the entry of Hard Rock and Rap music.

2016 (Best Singles)

1. "Love Yorself" Justin Bieber
2. "Sorry" Justin Bieber
3. "One Dance" Drake
4. "Work" Rihanna
5. "Stressed Out" Twenty One Pilots
6. "Panda" Designer
7. "Hello" Adele
8. "Don't Let Me Down" The Chainsmokers
9. "Can't Stop the Feeling" Justin Timberlake
10. "Closer" The Chainsomkers

1973 (Best Singles)

1. "Tie a Yellow Ribbon Round the Old Oak Tree"
    Tony Orlando and Dawn
2. "Bad, Bad Leroy Brown" Jim Croce
3. "Killing Me Softy" Roberta Flack
4. "Let's Get It On" Marvin Gaye
5. "My Love" Paul McCartney & Wings
6. "Why Me" Kris Kristofferson
7. "Crocodile Rock" Elton John
8. "Will It Go Round in Circles" Billy Preston
9. "You're So Vain" Carly Simon
10. "Touch Me in the Morning Diana Ross

1972 (Best Singles)

1. "The First Time Ever I Saw Your Face" Roberta Flack
2. "Alone Again (Naturally) Gilbert O'Sullivan
3. "American Pie" Don McLean
4. "Without You" Harry Nilsson
5. "The Candy Man" Sammy Davis Jr.
6. "I Gotcha" Joe Tex
7. "Lean on Me" Bill Withers
8. "Baby, Don't Get Hooked on Me" Mac Davis
9. "Brand New Key" Melanie
10. "Daddy Don't You Walk So Fast" Wayne Newton

1968 (Best Singles)

1. "Hey Jude" The Beatles
2. "Love is Blue" Paul Mauriat
3. "Honey" Bobby Goldsboro
4. "(Sittin' On) the Dock of the Bay" Otis Redding
5. "People Got to Be Free" The Rascals
6. "Sunshine of Your Love" Cream
7. "This Guys in Love With You" Herb Alpert
8. "The Good, the Bad and the Ugly" Hugo Montenegro
9. "Mrs. Robinson" Simon & Garfunkel
10. "Tighten Up" Archie Bell & the Drells

1965 (Best Singles)

1. "Wooly Bully" Sam the Sham and the Pharaohs
2. "I Can't Help Myself (Sugar Pie Honey Bunch) Four Tops
3. "(I Can't Get No) Satisfaction" The Rolling Stones
4. "You Were on My Mind" We Five
5. "You've Lost That Lovin' Feelin'" The Righteous Brothers
6. "Downtown" Petula Clark

7. "Help" The Beatles
8. "Can't You Hear My Heartbeat" Hermin's Hermits
9. "Crying in the Chapel" Elvis Presley
10. "My Girl" The Temptations

1957 (Best Singles)

1. "All Shook Up" Elvis Presey
2. "Love Letters in the Sand" Pat Boone
3. "Little Darlin'" The Diamonds
4. "Young Love" Tab Hunter
5. "So Rare" Jimmy Dorsey
6. "Don't Forbid Me" Pat Boone
7. "Singing the Blues" Guy Mitchell
8. "Young Love" Sonny James
9. "Too Much" Elvis Presley
10. "Round and Round" Perry Como

1952 (Best Singles)

1. "Blue Tango" Leroy Anderson
2. "Wheel of Fortune" Kay Starr
3. "Cry" Johnnie Ray & The Four Lads
4. "You Belong to Me" Jo Stafford
5. "Auf Wiederseh'n Sweetheart" Vera Lynn
6. "Half as Much" Rosemary Clooney
7. "Wish You Were Here" Eddie Fisher
8. "I Went to Your Wedding" Patti Page
9. "Here in My Heart" Al Martino
10. "Delicado" Percy Faith

1942 (Best Singles)

1. "White Christmas" Bing Crosdy
2. "(I've Got a Gal in) Kalamazoo Glenn Miller
3. "Tangerine" Jimmy Dorsey
4. "Moonlight Cocktail" Glenn Miller
5. "Sleepy Lagoon" Harry James
6. "(I Got Spurs That) Jingle, Jangle, Jingle Kay Kyser
7. "A String of Pearls" Glenn Miller
8. "Blues in the Night" Woody Herman
9. "Jersey Bounce" Benny Goodman
10. "Deep in the Heart of Texas" Alveno Ray

About the Author

Richard J. Bishirjian was Founding President and Professor of Government at Yorktown University from 2000-2016. He earned a B.A. from the University of Pittsburgh and a Ph.D. in Government and International Studies from the University of Notre Dame.

Dr. Bishirjian was Gerhart Niemeyer's teaching assistant at Notre Dame. He was an assistant professor in the Department of Politics at the University of Dallas in Texas, chairman of the Political Science Department at the College of New Rochelle in New York and founder of Yorktown University where he served as President and Professor of government from 2000-2016.

He served as a political appointee in the Reagan Administration and in the Administration of George H. W. Bush.

He is the editor of *A Public Philosophy Reader* and author of three books, *The Development of Political Theory*, *The Conservative Rebellion*, and *The Coming Death and Future Resurrection of American Higher Education*. His most recent work, *Coda*, is a novel published by En Route Books. His most recent three scholarly studies are *Ennobling Encounters, Rise and Fall of the American Empire,* and *Conscience and Power*. *Ennobling Encounters* was published by En Route Books in September, 2021.

Dr. Bishirjian's essays have been published in *Forbes*, *The Political Science Reviewer*, *Modern Age*, *Review of Politics*, *Chronicles,* the *American Spectator* and *The Imaginative Conservative*.

Made in the USA
Middletown, DE
30 May 2023

31165702R00136